WRITERS AN

ISOBEL /
Gener

C000225201

HANIF KUREISHI

© Jane Bown

HANIF KUREISHI

HANIF KUREISHI

RUVANI RANASINHA

Northcote House
in association with the
British Council

© Copyright 2002 by Ruvani Ranasinha

First published in 2002 by Northcote House Publishers Ltd, Horndon, Tavistock, Devon, PL19 9NQ, United Kingdom.
Tel: +44 (01822) 810066 Fax: +44 (01822) 810034.

All rights reserved. No part of this work may be reproduced or stored in an information retrieval system (other than short extracts for the purposes of review) without the express permission of the Publishers given in writing.

British Library Cataloguing in Publication Data
A catalogue record for this book is available from the British Library

ISBN 0-7463-0951-1

Typeset by PDQ Typesetting, Newcastle-under-Lyme
Printed and bound in Great Britain by
The Baskerville Press, Salisbury, Wiltshire, SP2 7QB

For
Amma and Thaththa
and for
Senani

Contents

Acknowledgements   viii

Biographical Outline   ix

Abbreviations   xii

Introduction: Situating Hanif Kureishi   1

1   Kureishi's Discovery of his Subject in his Early
    Plays: *Outskirts, Borderline* and *Birds of Passage*   21

2   The Politics of Representation: Political
    Commitment and Ironic Distance: *My Beautiful
    Laundrette* and *Sammy and Rosie Get Laid*   38

3   Culture and Identity: *The Buddha of Suburbia*   61

4   Muslimophobia: *The Black Album* and *My Son the
    Fanatic*   81

5   Mid-life Crisis – Variations on a Theme: *Love in
    a Blue Time, Intimacy, Sleep With Me* and *Midnight
    All Day*   102

Afterword   121

Notes   131

Select Bibliography   141

Index   145

Acknowledgements

I would like to thank Robert Young and Jon Mee for their engaged readings of earlier versions of this book and for inspiration and solicitude throughout this project. Conversations with Sara Salih and Qadri Ismail have helped shape my ideas. Thanks also to Hanif Kureishi for showing me his unpublished adaptation of Brecht's *Mother Courage and her Children*, manuscript of *Gabriel's Gift* and preface to the screenplay of *Intimacy* and for help with biographical information. Finally, my very special thanks to Senani and my family for their love and support.

Biographical Outline

1947	Rafiushan Kureishi leaves Bombay for England to study law. His Muslim family moves subsequently to the newly created Pakistan.
1954	Hanif Kureishi born in Bromley, Kent to Rafiushan Kureishi and Audrey Buss.
1958	Sister Yasmin born.
1965–1970	Kureishi attends Bromley Technical High School.
1971–3	Kureishi attends Ravensbourne College of Art for A-levels.
1974–7	Kureishi reads Philosophy at King's College, London. While attending university, Kureishi begins to work for the Royal Court Theatre.
1979	First play, *Soaking the Heat*, staged at the Royal Court Theatre Upstairs.
1980	January: *The King and Me* produced at the Soho Poly Theatre, directed by Antonia Bird.
	July: *The Mother Country* staged in the Riverside Studios' Plays Umbrella season.
1981	April: Kureishi wins the George Devine Award for *Outskirts*, first presented at the Royal Shakespeare's Company Warehouse Theatre. November: *Borderline* opens at the Royal Court Theatre, directed by Max Stafford-Clarke.
	Tomorrow-Today! performed at the Soho Poly Theatre London.
	Kureishi becomes Writer-in-Residence at the Royal Court.
1983	September: *Birds of Passage* opens at Hampstead Theatre, directed by Howard Davies.

1984	Adaptation of Brecht's *Mother Courage and Her Children* staged at the Barbican, directed by Howard Davies.
	February: Kureishi wrote *My Beautiful Laundrette* while visiting relatives in Karachi on his second visit to Pakistan.
1985	His first screenplay, *My Beautiful Laundrette,* released, directed by Stephen Frears. It receives an Oscar nomination for Best Original Screenplay and is nominated for BAFTA Best Screenplay Award. Wins New York Film Critics Best Screenplay Award.
1988	Kureishi's second screenplay, *Sammy and Rosie Get Laid,* released in Britain (released first in USA in 1987). The screenplay, together with Kureishi's diary about making the film with director Stephen Frears, published.
1989	Kureishi meets Tracey Scoffield, an editor at his publisher Faber and Faber.
1990	*The Buddha of Suburbia* published. Novel wins the Whitbread Award for the best first novel. It has been translated into over twenty-three languages.
1991	Release of film *London Kills Me,* written and directed by Kureishi.
	Kureishi's father dies.
1992	August: *London Kills Me* released in USA.
1993	Kureishi adapts *The Buddha of Suburbia* with Roger Michell for broadcast in the same year as a four-part BBC TV series, directed by Roger Michell.
1993	September–November: adaptation of *Mother Courage* produced as a mobile tour in the UK by the National Theatre's education department. December: production opens at the National Theatre.
1993	Twin sons Sachin and Carlo born to Tracey Scoffield and Kureishi.
1995	Second novel, *The Black Album,* published. *The Faber Book of Pop,* edited with Jon Savage, published.
1995	Kureishi leaves Tracey Scoffield.
1997	Collection of short stories *Love in a Blue Time* published. Screenplay *My Son the Fanatic* published.

1998	Film *My Son the Fanatic,* adapted by Kureishi from his short story released in Britain, directed by Udayan Prasad. Third novel *Intimacy* published.
1998	Son Kier born to Kureishi and Monique Proudlove.
1999	April: production of his play *Sleep with Me* opens at the Royal National Theatre, directed by Antony Page. November: second collection of short stories, *Midnight All Day* published.
2001	February: third novel, *Gabriel's Gift* published. July: Film of *Intimacy,* directed by Patrice Chéreau is released.

Abbreviations

BA   *The Black Album* (London: Faber and Faber, 1995)
BS   *The Buddha of Suburbia* (London: Faber and Faber, 1990)
F   *The Faber Book of Pop* (London: Faber and Faber, 1995)
G   *Gabriel's Gift* (London: Faber and Faber, 2001)
I   *Intimacy* (London: Faber and Faber, 1998)
LIBT   *Love in a Blue Time* (London: Faber and Faber, 1997)
LKM   *London Kills Me* (London: Faber and Faber, 1991)
MAD   *Midnight All Day* (London: Faber and Faber, 1999)
MBL   *My Beautiful Laundrette and Other Writings*, including 'The Rainbow Sign', 'Eight Arms to Hold You', 'Bradford', 'Wild Women, Wild Men', 'Finishing the Job' (London: Faber and Faber, 1996)
MSF   *My Son the Fanatic* (London: Faber and Faber, 1997)
OAOP   *Outskirts and Other Plays*, including *The King and Me, Outskirts, Borderline, Birds of Passage* (London: Faber and Faber, 1992)
SRGL   *Sammy and Rosie Get Laid*, including 'Some Time With Stephen: A Diary' (London: Faber and Faber, 1988)
SWM   *Sleep With Me* (London: Faber and Faber, 1999)

Introduction:
Situating Hanif Kureishi

Anglo-Pakistani Hanif Kureishi's vivid evocations of a multi-cultural, post-colonial London, peopled by sexually liberated protagonists redefined British cinema and invigorated the British novel. In his plays, screenplays and fiction he articulated and popularized British Asian experiences that had previously received marginal cultural representation and asserted their place in the nation. This book evaluates Kureishi's artistic development and achievement over the last two decades. It examines why this versatile author is one of the most celebrated, entertaining chroniclers of Britain's shifting racialized boundaries and changing sexual and political mores.

A NEW WAY OF BEING BRITISH

I want to begin with Kureishi's autobiographical essay 'The Rainbow Sign' (1986) because it directs us to his political purpose and gestures towards the ambivalence of his subject position that inflects his writing. We find an explicit statement of his initial project. Writing and intervening in public debates in the 1980s, he wants to explore 'a new way of being British', and reconfigure dominant, exclusive constructions of Britain in the context of large-scale post-war immigration (MBL 102).[1] He argues 'It is the British, the white British, who have to learn that being British isn't what it was. Now it is a more complex thing, involving new elements' (MBL 101-2).[2] Kureishi's art does not simply signal the presence of minority 'ethnic' communities, or merely assert their right to equal citizenship. It emphasizes how

1

these 'new elements' are transforming what it means to be British, contesting monocultural constructions of British identity. He is defining and shaping contemporary British hybridized culture.

In clear and compelling prose, the essay charts his political socialization. The author begins with his adolescence as a 'mixed race' youth growing up in xenophobic white suburbia when Enoch Powell was inciting racial tensions in the mid-sixties and prophesying racial war.[3] Kureishi discovered that his mixed Pakistani and English parentage identifies him structurally and racially as black in Britain. His racialized identity is defined in a corporeal way. His skin colour is a visible signifier of difference in white Britain, a negative identity given 'the brutal absurdity of racial classification'.[4] 'The Rainbow Sign' reveals the different forms of racist abuse that Kureishi experienced which infuse his work.[5] It marks his movement from an internalization of inferiority to anger and protest. At first he observes, 'I was desperately embarrassed and afraid of being identified with these loathed aliens. I found it almost impossible to answer questions about where I came from. The word "Pakistani" had been made into an insult. It was a word I didn't want used about myself' (MBL 76). But this racial location served both to 'oppress' and 'radicalize' Kureishi.[6] Cut off from minority communities, reading about the increasingly militant nature of the American Civil Rights Movement of the 1960s, he became inspired by the defiant, combative resistance to white racism of the Black Panthers. 'The Rainbow Sign' recounts Kureishi's growing awareness that his black identity has a political dimension.[7]

This polemical essay embodies the key themes that fuel much of Kureishi's early work: racism and possible responses to it. Kureishi exposes the Orwellian complacency and faith in a tolerant British society as a widely acclaimed but false belief.[8] It does not take into account the 'violence, hostility and contempt directed against black people every day by the state and individual alike' (MBL 101). He wants to shock his readers into an awareness of racism, a subject he tenaciously explores in his work, albeit in a more ironic and comic mode. In this serious, powerful, eloquent indictment of race relations in Britain, Kureishi situates himself between two absolutes, the Right of the National Front and the British National Party, and the

2

separatist positions of some anti-racists. He dismisses the monocultural imperatives of assimilation as the majority's attempt to control, remake or efface the minority culture: 'The British complained incessantly that the Pakistanis wouldn't assimilate. This meant they wanted the Pakistanis to be exactly like them' (*MBL* 76). At the same time, Kureishi is equally emphatic in his rejection of the separatism advocated by Elijah Muhammed and Malcolm X. Kureishi critiques any form of anti-racism which constructs itself in terms of a similar exclusive separatism: 'And the separatism, the total loathing of the white man as innately corrupt, the "All whites are devils" view, was...unacceptable. I had to live in England, in the suburbs of London, with whites. My mother was white. I wasn't ready for separate development. I'd had too much of that already' (*MBL* 78). Instead, Kureishi identifies with Richard Wright and James Baldwin who were opposed both to white racism and to the separatist Muslim movement the Nation of Islam. Kureishi's distrust of separatism and Islamic 'fundamentalism' is a preoccupation that resurfaces throughout his creative work, as we will see. His work traces the fractured nature of contemporary British society. Kureishi's statement reveals the degree to which his mixed descent relates to his politics: he feels it makes only certain options thinkable for him. What emerges is that the racializing of identity is particularly problematic for the subject whose racial identity is not clear-cut: it underlines the instability and indeterminacy of race as a category. A mixed descent exacerbates the notion of choice and of belonging in neither community, and is riven by ambivalence, labile and mutable identities.

'The Rainbow Sign' points to other ambivalences. Relating Kureishi's first visit to Pakistan where he confronts his multiple identities and locations, it discusses the concepts of 'home' and 'belonging' – tropes that recur in his work. Kureishi's identification with Pakistan is not straightforward. Kureishi's father (like Salman Rushdie) grew up in Bombay and never lived in Pakistan, moving to England in 1947, the year India became independent and Pakistan was created, when the extended family moved to Karachi. Consequently in interviews Kureishi refers to his paternal relations as Indian and Pakistani interchangeably. Kureishi feels his stay in Pakistan helped him

3

regain the 'fragments' of his past which include 'Bombay' and 'Delhi': this underlines the construction of an imaginary diasporic identity (*MBL* 99). Enamoured by his warm reception in Pakistan, he is conscious of what he sees as the pitfalls of giving in to the 'falsity' and 'sentimentality' of feeling 'too Pakistani' (*MBL* 81). The trip to Pakistan was a defining experience for Kureishi: 'It is strange to go away to the land of your ancestors, to find out how much you have in common with people there, yet at the same time to realize how British you are... what little choice you have in the matter of your background and where you belong' (*MBL* 99–100).

Kureishi expresses his attachment to Britain and its freedoms defined (in a rather West-centric way) in contrast to 'the illiberalism and lack of possibility of Pakistan' (*MBL* 99). Yet a complete, unambiguous identification remains fraught in the face of continuing white racism – at times, he feels 'who wants to be British anyway?' (*MBL* 100). Throughout the essay, Kureishi veers between alienation and identification. Repelled by right-wing attempts to construct England as the exclusive domain of hegemonic white ethnicity, Kureishi observes, 'I have never wanted to identify with England. When Enoch Powell spoke for England I turned away in final disgust.' However 'despite all this, some kind of identification with England remains' (*MBL* 99). This issue of citizenship remains fraught. Often he prefers to locate himself in cosmopolitan London: 'I'm a Londoner, not a Brit.'[9] Many black Britons prefer to describe themselves as 'British' citizens rather than as 'English':[10] the latter is more overtly imbricated in exclusive monocultural terms to signify whiteness. In contrast, Kureishi and his characters identify themselves primarily with Englishness. Anuradha Dingwaney Needham suggests that the meanings that cluster around the term 'British' are more suitable for his political project.[11] However what clearly concerns Kureishi is the way both terms are used problematically to exclude. He asserts his claim to the aspects of Britishness *and* Englishness that he admires. As Simon Gikandi argues, Kureishi's identification is based on the belief that he can 'valorize the logic of a secular and enlightened English culture and use it against the unreason of the racists'.[12] Although, we will see in chapter 4 concerning Kureishi's portrayals of British Muslims, this 'logic' is not so straightforward.

Kureishi emphasizes the degree to which he is shaped and 'formed by England' (*MBL* 100). Here as elsewhere his work consistently shows that although he is positioned as an outsider he is very much an insider. His irony, his dissection of British class antagonisms, and his immersion in popular culture all signal his 'Englishness'. His work is peopled with characters that resist being defined according to their ethnicity and labelled as irreconcilably 'different'. In the same way, his moves between genres and styles parallel his attempts to find freedom of identity outside formal definitions. Similarly, Kureishi rightly refuses to limit himself to the subjects marked for minority writers: the requirement to discuss matters of race in his work. He asserts his right to comment on wider themes and British society and culture from his own aesthetic point of view, which is in his case a quizzical, ironic perspective. While this essay distils Kureishi's politics, what is missing is the pervasive humour and irony with which he treats serious issues, that characterizes his work. Kureishi is explicit in this essay. This contrasts with his more customary refusal to be situated in one position: this ambivalence and ironic distance makes his work more difficult to interpret politically. His irony is itself a refusal to commit. This validation of uncertainty, resistance to totalizing narratives and concern with the relativity of perception are embodied in different ways in the various genres he employs. The farcical elements of his early plays and novels, and the anti-naturalist effects of his early screenplays fracture the surface realism of his work. Kureishi locates his distrust of 'pure' or unproblematic realism in terms of the impact of 1960s pop culture: 'the first lesson of LSD was that reality was something more evanescent and fugitive than most of us imagined for a long time' (*F*, p. xviii).

FROM POST-COLONIALISM TO MULTICULTURALISM

Although this was not always the case, today, within Britain, Kureishi is usually referred to as a British writer. Post-colonial literary and cultural studies examine Kureishi's work more specifically in the category of black British writing.[13] His texts are also sometimes subsumed under categories of 'migrant writing' and 'post-independence Indian writing in English'.[14] Kureishi contests such positioning insisting, 'I'm not a Pakistani or an Indian writer, I'm a British writer'.[15] These conflicting designations raise questions that are central to Kureishi's emphasis on the importance of rethinking what it means to be British. For it is only in a truly plural Britain that Kureishi can straightforwardly be British or a British writer and accepted as indisputably belonging.[16] Such debates have not died down.[17]

Migrant narratives of acculturation describe now transplanted subjectivities formed during different stages of the colonial and decolonized history of the former colonies. These are very different from the narrativized experiences (most explicitly in *The Buddha of Suburbia*) of a writer who grows up in a south London suburb, whose father happens to be Pakistani. The popular assumption is that such people are still migrants in some sense: hence Kureishi's objection to the term 'second-generation immigrants' on the grounds that it ensures 'that there was no mistake about our not really belonging in Britain' (*MBL* 134–5). Kureishi contests such exclusion. He asserts that the cultural situation is very different. The extent to which an individual like Kureishi will absorb anything other than the current British culture of his or her peers depends on several factors. The key conditions are the attitude of the parents, their own background (rural or cosmopolitan) and the degree to which he or she is brought up in an 'ethnic' local community such as Bradford in contrast to white suburban Kent. Kureishi never heard Urdu at home, because his father's first language was English, and he describes his father's family as anglophone, anglophile, and 'alien even in India'.[18] For Kureishi brought up by a white British mother, in white suburbia, largely isolated from Pakistani communities, the 'Asian' dimension of his ethnic identity will be a defining experience but not the only one or even *the* defining experience. In an interview in the *New York Times*, Kureishi describes his upbringing and intellectual formation as monocultural:

> 'I was brought up really as an English child...my father was very Westernized – he wasn't a practising Muslim, for example, he didn't believe in arranged marriages or practices that would have conflicted with what was around us. I wasn't influenced by Asian culture at all.'[19]

The overstatement in the last line is perhaps a response to being repeatedly categorized in essentialist terms. While Kureishi is not obviously syncretic in intellectual formation, in the sense of incorporating subcontinental subjects or forms like Rushdie, at the same time he is influenced by Asian culture. He shares the same cultural references of his white British peers and yet his exposure to, for example, his Pakistani and British Asian relations, provides him with an added dimension. This perspective is both similar to and not the same as Edward Said's 'contrapuntal' awareness of intellectuals situated on cultural borders or Rushdie's 'stereoscopic' vision. Steeped in mainstream British culture, Kureishi's work is marked by the split awareness of the minority artist.[20]

Kureishi's writings form a complex relationship to early black writers who first came to Britain from Africa, the Caribbean or the Indian subcontinent as migrants. His black 'precursors' have long engaged with the challenges of living in Britain in the face of racial hostility. While there is an overlap of concerns, Kureishi is articulating a very different experience. Examining the ways Kureishi's work is both aligned to and different from these writers enables a clearer assessment of his achievement. Kureishi's work can be located in relation to first-generation writers and theorists Stuart Hall, Homi Bhabha and Salman Rushdie's theorizing of post-colonial migration to the metropolis as the subversion of the centre at its very heart both culturally and demographically. This deconstruction of dominant configurations of the nation is tied up with Bhabha and Rushdie's celebration of the liberatory potential of cultural hybridity, which Kureishi's work both embodies and complicates.[21] Similarly, the impulse of many first-generation migrants to 'write back' to the centre from within is reflected in Kureishi's work. Like Rushdie's *The Satanic Verses*, *The Buddha of Suburbia* demythologizes the 'mother' country by strategies of inversion through the eyes of its first-generation protagonist Haroon Amir. Haroon is 'amazed and heartened by the sight of the British in England...He'd never seen the English in poverty, as road-sweepers, dustmen, shopkeepers and barmen. He'd never seen an Englishman stuffing bread into his mouth with his fingers, and no one had told him the English didn't wash regularly because the water was so cold – if they had water at all' (*BS* 24). However, the emphasis of Kureishi's work is predominately on the contemporary results of immigration reconfiguring British culture and with mapping today's multicultural Britain, along with a host of other writers including Timothy Mo, Joan Riley, Caryl Phillips, Merle Collins, Meera Syal, Diran Adebayo and Zadie Smith. While this emphasis may seem to be epitomized by Rushdie's hybridized post-colonial London, Rushdie's hybridization takes a different form to Kureishi's. Rushdie hybridizes the 'English' novel in style and form, fusing indigenous Indian literary sources such as *The Mahabharata* with Laurence Sterne and Henry Fielding as a form of cultural contestation. In contrast, Kureishi's writing does not draw on Pakistani and Indian literary influences. Unlike Rushdie, he does not experiment with varieties of English and linguistic hybridity. Although Kureishi's prose invigorates Standard English with the Indian English speech of some of his characters, and the incorporation of literal translations of Urdu swear words in *The Buddha of Suburbia*, the Indian English is always contained in the dialogue as a form of characterization. Narration remains in British English. Kureishi does not attempt to subvert the hierarchy of Englishes: he is not 'remaking English' in the manner of Rushdie and G. V. Desani before him.[22] If Kureishi does transgress notions of Standard English it is in his unrestrained use of colloquialisms, swear words and sexually explicit language which have become his trademark.[23]

Previous authors such as Sam Selvon and V. S. Naipaul have narrated the story of arrival in Britain from the former colonies. Many of them were already familiar with forms of English culture mediated through English Literature that dominated their colonial education, fostering feelings of alienation in their own country. This is Kureishi's father's experience. Kureishi's early narratives re-examine the first-generation immigrants' story of arrival and the different ways they have adapted to life in Britain. His work emphasizes the differences between first generation immigrants' and their children's relationship to the 'host' and 'home' countries, and in their values and beliefs, and the impact on identity-formation of their different formative experiences.

Both Rushdie and Naipaul have described the shock on arrival (as anglicized Asians from ex-colonies) of being perceived as alien in the 'mother' country. However, as Rushdie suggests,

8

'At least I know that I really am a foreigner, and don't feel very English. I don't define myself by nationality – my passport doesn't tell me who I am'.[24] For the generation who were born or grew up in Britain this sense of exclusion is felt more acutely and very differently. As Kureishi observes, 'But for me and the others of my generation born here, Britain was always where we belonged, even when were told – often in terms of racial abuse – that this was not so' (MBL 135). So Kureishi differs from older writers in being among the first to articulate what it is like to feel British, grow up in Britain and be regarded as alien. This disjunction between how Kureishi sees himself as a Londoner and how wider society perceives him is a formative influence that animates his work. The Buddha of Suburbia turns on the ironies that emerge from these conflicting viewpoints. His masterly ability to politicize the personal allows his work to point beyond the contradictions of his particular subject position staging the issues in terms of a re-writing of post-colonial Britain. His work, like that of his peers such as Linton Kwesi Johnson's poetry, defiantly contests exclusionary attitudes.

Kureishi's attitude towards London invites further comparison with early black writers. In a perceptive essay delineating Kureishi's cartography of London, Sukhdev Sandhu contrasts Naipaul's reverential attitude to London and poignant desire to 'find the centre' and its supposed 'stability and assurances' with Kureishi's, who revels in London's 'disruptions and upheavals'.[25] Kureishi's fascination with inner London's 'fluidity and possibilities' equally differs from first-generation migrant Nirad Chaudhuri's search for 'Timeless England' (SRGL 101). In contrast to these first-generation writers, Kureishi and his protagonists negotiate a differently classed trajectory from the provincial margins of suburban tedium to the centrality of the cultural capital. Almost all Kureishi's work is set in and around London, which he calls his 'playground'.[26] Defined against suburbia, London represents much more than the backdrop of his work. It is central to Kureishi's purpose and politics: his sustained exposure of its underbelly, dereliction and violence, as well as his celebration of its freedoms, potential for self-reinvention and energizing creativity. His protagonists' escape from the suburbs to the metropolis is key to their self-development.[27] Like Rushdie, Kureishi extols a hybridized post-colonial London with its multicultural possibilities: hence Kureishi's early self-positioning as 'a Londoner, not a Brit'.

MULTIPLE INHERITANCES

Kureishi's pervasive ironizing, scepticism and satirical humour underline the extent to which his work is steeped in what might be regarded as English traditions of social criticism and political analysis through irony and satire. Kureishi emphasizes the 'tradition that I come from in Britain is really the Royal Court Theat[re]. It's really a tradition of dissent, of making plays and films and stories, which are arguments about British society'.[28] Recently critics, following Kureishi's lead and perhaps to support his claim to 'Englishness', foreground this aspect of his 'genealogy'. A notable example is Kenneth Kaleta's critical biography. Kaleta positions Kureishi's 'brutal wit' and 'anger' in the English theatrical tradition, continuing a line from Richard Sheridan to John Osborne: one of the abrasive, alienated writers and dramatists known as the 'Angry Young Men' of the 1950s. Kaleta suggests that 'Joe Orton's irreverent plays set in Sixties London are the most proximate ancestor in English playwriting of Kureishi's London plays'.[29] Indeed, Orton's anarchic humour subversive of all forms of authority resonates in Kureishi's work. Possible 'English' sources are endless. John Braine's ambitious, desiring, cynical Joe Lampton, making his way in *Room at the Top* (1957), prefigures Karim in Kureishi's *Bildungsroman The Buddha of Suburbia*.

In the same vein, Alamgir Hashmir argues that critics ignore the 'dual tradition' of Kureishi's fiction. Hashmir suggests that in *The Buddha of Suburbia* while the 'quality of humour, particularly the sarcasm, are distinctly Pakistani', the 'plebeian manner is worn with a panache that only a literary culture with a working-class tradition – such as Britain's – can make possible'. Hashmir situates Kureishi in the tradition of the English comic novel and examines his debt to H. G. Wells. Hashmir suggests Kureishi shares with Wells and other British novelists a 'social realism enlivened and relieved by a sure comicality'. As well as an interest in 'suburban drolls, social

10

mores, and people on the make, with a keen eye to their oddities and peculiarities'. He goes on to suggest that the 'farcical elements' in Kureishi's work resemble Angus Wilson's fiction and that, in common with many post-war English writers, Kureishi is concerned with 'the ennui, struggles and antics of the underclass' in search of personal fulfilment.[30] These elements are without doubt present in Kureishi's work. My own emphasis on Kureishi's post-colonial black forerunners is not to undermine the extent to which his work is permeated and shaped by white-authored texts. However, Kureishi's eclectic borrowings attest to the futility of tracing literary influences and situating writers in terms of false 'national' homogeneous traditions.

Kureishi's intellectual formation is moulded by many cross-cultural, transnational influences, including as we have seen black American writers but also Frantz Fanon. He draws on the intellectual cross-fertilizations of what Paul Gilroy defines as 'a black Atlantic' an 'intercultural and transnational formation' that suggests the degree to which African-American, British and Caribbean diasporic cultures have mutually influenced each other and their metropolitan bases.[31] Equally, Kureishi acknowledges the influence of white American writers J. D. Salinger, Philip Roth, Saul Bellow and Norman Mailer, 'who were writing about contemporary life in a way that British writers weren't'.[32] The sexual explicitness of Roth's writing and its complex relationship with his Jewish background and portrayals of contemporary Jewish life that aroused similar controversy have obvious resonances with Kureishi's work. As does Salinger's racy, idiomatic dialogue and appeal to the young. The emphasis on pop and drug culture suggests Kureishi's debt to writers Jack Kerouac and John Updike.

CULTURAL TRANSLATION AND THE POLITICS OF REPRESENTATION

Just as first-generation migrant writers were positioned as 'authentic' insiders and translators of Eastern *countries*, at the outset of his career Kureishi was constructed as a privileged insider and translator of minority *communities* who live in Britain. Critical responses to first-generation writers such as

11

Naipaul and Rushdie have addressed the politics of their reconstitution of the foreign country for the target western audience. The post-colonial migrant genre is examined as a creative space where dominant notions of the 'Third' World and the 'First' worlds are juxtaposed, challenged and reinforced. With Kureishi's generation, the problem of Orientalist portrayals of Eastern cultures to the West is transmuted to one of the politics of representing the minority communities to the dominant gaze of the majority community, as well as to an increasing minority readership or viewership. Again, minority art is examined in terms of the way it reinforces and militates against dominant ideologies and perceptions of minorities.

Kureishi recalls how his writing career began as a cultural translator. He suggests his early work was materially produced in the 'politically conscious seventies, [when] there was, in TV and theatre, a liberal desire to encourage work from unmapped and emergent areas.... They required stories about the new British communities, by cultural translators, as it were, to interpret one side to the other' (*OAOP*, pp. xv–xvi). Kureishi admits that at the time he was happy to assume the position assigned without unpacking its implications. 'I didn't think much about whether I was the sort of writer best-suited to this kind of work; I just knew I was being paid to write' (*OAOP*, pp. xviii). A hallmark of Kureishi's work is the way he both exploits and resists his ethnic identity. His early complicity with this role is ironic in that much of his own work questions some of the problematic implications or pitfalls of cultural translation.

The problem with traditional conceptions of cultural translation is the implicit assumption that the two cultures undergoing translation are discrete entities sealed off from one another.[33] Kureishi undoes this assumption, underlining the extent to which the histories of the subcontinent and Britain are ineluctably intertwined and continue to be so despite the separation of decolonization. In 'Pakistan, Britain just wouldn't go away', writes Kureishi, 'The two countries...have been part of each other for years, usually to the advantage of Britain. They cannot now be wrenched apart, even if that were desirable. Their futures will be intermixed (*MBL* 91, 102). This applies to the second generation's 'hybrid' identities. Kureishi avers that notions of Asian and British cannot be defined separately. His

12

protagonists live the potentials and experience the pitfalls of mixing and métissage. His work parodies the idea of homogeneous, distinct racially defined communities. Secondly, cultural translation can privilege the notion of an authentic insider and valorize the 'original'. Kureishi's texts repudiate any claims to represent authentic or representative portraits.

Kureishi's role as cultural translator can be more usefully examined with reference to JanMohamed's model of intellectuals on cultural borders. However, JanMohamed's concept refers to the interior/exterior position that first-generation *migrants* occupy on cultural borders. Unlike JanMohamed's border intellectuals, Kureishi's generation are not 'migrants' nor have they been physically translated. In their mediation between the majority and minority community, the British-born generation occupies a different position on the insider/outsider spectrum, one of internal syncretism as hybrid insiders.[34] Kureishi thematizes this insider/outsider location in his work: his British Asian and 'mixed race' protagonists are described as 'in-betweens' (*MBL* 20). What is useful about JanMohamed's model is his use of the term 'specular' to denote the way certain border intellectuals act as mirrors in 'reflecting' their context. In the same way that cultural translation is never a neutral, unmediated or transparent representation of a culture or community, JanMohamed invests specular border intellectuals on cultural margins with a reflective potential, a specular potentiality that is equally *mediated*. (The *OED* defines specular: 'Of vision: Obtained by reflection only; not direct or immediate.') Just as cultural translation both contests and reinforces the expectations of sections of the recipient dominant culture, JanMohamed values border intellectuals' ability to contest uncritical, affirming reflections of the dominant host culture. They militate against dominant representations by 'mirroring analytically' the host culture's 'own hidden ideological procedures and programs'.[35] At the same time, JanMohamed warns that these border intellectuals have to guard themselves against what he calls 'the traps of specularity'. That is when border intellectuals who are not 'sitting' on the border but are 'forced *to constitute themselves as the border* reflect the "identity" and "homogeneity" of the group that constructed it'.[36] Nirad Chaudhuri would seem to be an example of a migrant

13

intellectual who falls into the trap of specularity: he articulates and affirms hegemonic notions of 'Englishness', in contrast to Rushdie who endeavours to challenge it.

This book examines the ways in which Kureishi occupies or performs this specular role. The term 'specular' is a particularly apt description of Kureishi for two reasons. First, his works register with such precision the era in which they are set, often departing from conventional representations, instead revisiting its *Zeitgeist*, its desires, conflicts and contradictions. Secondly, his pervasive ironizing perspective performs a specular function in his satirical representations of British Asians and white British. This book is concerned with the following questions. To what degree do Kureishi's texts exemplify and/or resist the 'trap of specularity'? In what ways does his work critically reflect the majority and minority communities? How far does it question or challenge dominant ideologies and perceptions and to what extent does it embody them? It is important to remember that although Kureishi is 'translating' minority communities, in also delineating the majority community Kureishi (like other black writers) inverts the dominant 'gaze'. As Coco Fusco suggests, 'To ignore white ethnicity is to redouble its hegemony by naturalising it. Without specifically addressing white ethnicity, there can be no critical evaluation of the construction of the other.'[37] In this way, the specular role can be a subversive assertion of equality. To differing degrees, Kureishi's texts destabilize the opposition between dominant 'gaze' and object. The scattered multiple viewpoints in his novels and the disruption of realism in his films offer counter-discursive perspectives by highlighting the process of interpellation.

Unlike first-generation immigrant writers who tend to focus on conflicts *between* cultures, Kureishi and other British-born writers 'reflect' discord between generations and *within* communities. Kureishi's texts demonstrate that identities cannot be exclusively considered in terms of cultural difference, but need to be examined in relation to other differences of generation, class, gender and sexual orientation. Kureishi's work draws attention to how these constructs impinge on the contested issue of what it means to be of Asian origin in Britain. He disrupts simple, fixed notions of identity and the monolithic, static nature of immigrant experience. Along with a range of black artists, his portrayals

14

break decisively from reactive, defensive representations and 'the stifling aesthetic of the positive image'.[38] Instead he shows the complexity and diversity of the lives and experiences of Asian people in Britain. The emphasis on humorous, plural self-definitions rather than an exclusive focus on refuting white stereotypes, is characteristic of Kureishi's representations. In contrast to first-generation artists, Kureishi's generation with greater access to diverse, public media develop their aesthetic and political responses through public forms of representation such as drama, film and TV. This led to debates on the 'burden' of the politics of representing a community that attend such widely circulated texts. Kureishi's portrayals provoked especial controversy and fuelled such debates.

POPULAR CULTURE

Kureishi's plays, screenwriting and fiction, immersed in popular culture, contrast with the more narrowly literary writings of earlier writers from a post-colonial background. British pop music, with its roots in American music and youth culture, Kureishi notes 'was always a part of my cultural vocabulary – far more than anything more esoteric'.[39] For Kureishi, pop was the 'first sort of common culture that [he] was ever aware of'.[40] His texts are permeated by transatlantic youth culture, not the Bollywood films informing Rushdie's novels or Meera Syal and Gurinder Chadha's *Bhaji on the Beach* (1993). Kureishi breaks the conventions of realism but not by using 'Asian' influences. This 'Englishness' redefines expectations about the writing and culture of minority artists. In his introduction to *The Faber Book of Pop* (co-edited with Jon Savage) Kureishi's characterization of pop writing underscores the extent to which the themes he identifies are those that inflect his own work. 'Pop provided writers with new areas to explore', writes Kureishi, 'writing about pop introduces us to the fringes of the respectable world, to marijuana, generational conflict, clubs, parties, and to a certain kind of guiltless, casual sex that had never been written about before' (F, p. xix). It is in this 'fringe world' of city culture that Kureishi's work is located, imbuing it with its distinctive metropolitan, hip quality.

15

Kureishi's emphasis on pop is neither unconnected nor in a contradictory relation to his ethnic location: in the sixties and seventies youth subcultures and ethnic cultures were both positioned in a marginal and contestatory relationship to the dominant culture, although they were also situated against each other. Clearly influenced by Dick Hebdige's work, *The Faber Book of Pop* underscores youth culture's subversive potential, citing Stuart Hall:

> popular culture always has its base in the experiences, the pleasures, the memories, the traditions of the people.... Hence, it links with what Mikhail Bakhtin calls 'the vulgar' – the popular, the informal, the underside, the grotesque. That is why it has always been counterposed to elite or high culture, and is thus a site of alternative traditions. And that is why the dominant tradition has always been afraid of it, quite rightly.' (F 669)

The Faber Book of Pop celebrates the way pop culture undermined the dominant class's stranglehold on exclusive visibility. The diversity of pop is examined in terms of the way that it 'continues to grant visibility and audibility to voices often excluded from the mainstream – Afro-Caribbeans, homosexuals, women, outsiders of all types' (F, p. xxxiii). The anthology foregrounds pop's role in shaping attitudes towards sexuality, gender, race and class. Today, as Alison Donnell observes, 'it is more difficult to locate subcultures as situated in opposition to dominant culture in the same way as they were twenty years ago when Dick Hebdige published his influential study *Subculture: The Meaning of Style* (1979)'.[41] Similarly Kureishi and Savage present pop in the sixties as at its most subversive, although their final section on pop from 1988 to 'The end of the century' includes extracts which 'highlight pop as a site of continuing struggle' (F 672). All Kureishi's screenplays have powerful soundtracks, and his fiction incorporates many references to pop songs in his recreation of specific eras. 'Funny too', writes Kureishi, 'how much it can tell us about a particular period, as if it's the easily forgotten things that we most need to recover' (F, p. xx). In his coming of age narratives *The Buddha of Suburbia* and *The Black Album*, 'visceral', 'sensual' pop songs are invoked to register the 'exhilaration' and 'momentary but powerful impulse' the 'teenage sexual longing' of his libidinous fictional protagonists (F, p. xix). In Kureishi's work mutable, fluid, ethnic,

16

gendered and sexual identities are explored in terms of the ephemeral, transitory nature of youth culture. Kureishi is a self-proclaimed child of the sixties: 'I saw the sixties on TV and was formed by what I missed out on'. His beliefs that 'openness and choice in sexual behaviour is liberating' and that there should be 'fluid, non-hierarchical society' stem from the era's radical aspirations (*SRGL* 77). While his work is informed by the sixties liberatory counter-cultural movements, anti-authoritarianism, sex, drugs, music and radical politics, it is more directly contextualized in the seventies, eighties and nineties. Increasingly his work reflects hedonistic seventies and eighties culture without the concomitant political commitment, such as the liberated, but directionless couple Sammy and Rosie. Kureishi has described *London Kills Me* (1991) as reflecting the individualism of the eighties, where the drug scene resembled the sixties culture of hedonism only without the politics.[42] In *The Black Album*, Deedee a former Marxist, abandons political commitment for a liberal sensualism. This trajectory is partly in keeping with his role as chronicler 'reflecting' the contemporary shift from macro to micro-politics. Kureishi comments that 'if Britain feels pleasantly hedonistic and politically torpid, it might be because the...politics of personal relationships has replaced that of a society, which seems uncontrollable'.[43] This movement also points to Kureishi's own political orientation and direction. As we will see, in his work, 'politics' and 'desire' both collude and collide: sexual pleasure is simultaneously politicized and in tension with political commitment.

Kureishi's oeuvre can be broadly divided into two phases. Questions of race, class, gender and sexuality explored from a progressive perspective form the central debates of almost all of Kureishi's work from his early plays until *Love in a Blue Time* (1997).[44] He foregrounds sexual desire and pleasure. His protagonists are identified and identify themselves by fluid sexual identities, which are presented as potentially liberating, transgressing race and class divisions. His male and female characters deploy sex to contest prescribed gender roles and oppose reductive attempts to categorize them according to ethnic boundaries. While Kureishi politicizes sex and sexual relationships, at the same time the emphasis on sex deflects

17

attention from other forms of politics and distracts his protagonists from political commitments and action. This is particularly evident in *Sammy and Rosie Get Laid*. Kureishi's work dramatizes the ways in which sexual pleasure complicates and renders cultural identification and political engagement ambivalent and unstable.

This first phase stages a series of choices according to pre-defined categories. Kureishi's texts posit various forms of individualism against communal modes of solidarity. The *OED* definitions of individualism point to its negative and positive connotations: 'Self-centred feeling or conduct as principle' and 'a free and independent individual'. Kureishi's male protagonists embody both aspects, which accounts for their ambivalence. In his early play *Borderline*, Haroon rejects the Asian Youth Front's separatist activism to pursue his career as a lawyer.[45] In *The Buddha of Suburbia*, defined in contrast to Jamila whose brand of individualism remains politically engaged, Karim espouses a form of liberal individualism that evades political commitment to the anti-racist movement. In *The Black Album* Shahid chooses liberal sensualism over Islamic 'fundamentalism' *and* anti-racism.

Kureishi's protagonists' ambivalence about 'belonging' to an 'ethnic' community is presented to differing degrees as a healthy scepticism and assertion of independence or resistance to oppressive forms of identification stemming from notions of community based around ethnicity. However, Kureishi often elides such resistance with a rejection of political commitment. In terms of the polarities Kureishi sets up, the rejection of the group often involves a concomitant dismissal of modes of political solidarity. Yet, as Jamila's independence shows, as a member of a 'collective' based on ideological not ethnic ties, anti-racism does not necessarily involve an uncritical identification with an ethnic community.

Kureishi's male protagonists tend to reflect the opposing factions that surround them: but at the core, there is a nullity; they remain spectral and specular figures with no strong sense of self. They form a series of often engaging hedonists who ultimately privilege their personal goals. This is a stance Kureishi appears to both endorse and critique. Incrementally his work appears to privilege individualism and disengagement,

18

although the extent to which he is thematizing this as failure or naturalizing it remains open to question. The conflicting discourses and competing voices articulated in his work and the pervasive ironizing of all positions, even individualism, are integral to Kureishi's ambivalence and complexity. Kureishi's ironic distance enables him to avoid closure or resolution. He leaves it for the reader or viewer to decide.

In the novels and short stories *Love in a Blue Time*, *Intimacy*, *Midnight All Day* and his play *Sleep With Me* that comprise his second phase, race is no longer the central focus. What remains from his earlier work is Kureishi's emphasis on sexual desire. His protagonists' self-absorbed passion that always threatened to disrupt the overtly 'political' content seems eventually to triumph in his recent explorations of the nuances of personal relationships and the complexity of sexuality. However, I would argue that the shift from race to intimate relationships is not a new direction but a more explicit examination of Kureishi's latent preoccupations with diverse forms of masculinity and different kinds of relationships. *My Beautiful Laundrette* both exemplifies this link and anticipates these later concerns in its exploration of *the question of race through sexuality and constructions of masculinity.*

Kureishi has always been interested in sexual relationships, friendships and family relationships – especially those between fathers and sons; mothers tend to be absent or marginalized and often depressed, inert figures. Although Kureishi's early texts revolve around overtly politicized positions, they also explore the more nebulous implications of 'belonging' that resurface in a more pronounced form in these later works. He is concerned with what being part of a social formation (whether it be an ethnic community or family) involves. His characters are not making these choices from a neutral space. They are already both an individual and a member of a group; they cannot wholly extricate themselves from any of these groups. The choice is really one of how to define oneself within the group and balance competing demands between self and others. The tension between the communal and the individual is at the heart of all Kureishi's work. Ethnicity and masculinity are both paradigms of constructing identity that Kureishi's protagonists both participate in and attempt to resist in order to assert their autonomy. Kureishi's foremost protagonists Haroon, Karim and Shahid are all independent individualists who distance themselves from commitments to others. Similarly Kureishi presents Jay in *Intimacy* resisting relations of duty to his family that are incompatible with his individual freedom and desires. Characteristically Kureishi constructs this as both selfish *and* a necessary, essential assertion of autonomy.

1

Kureishi's Discovery of his Subject in his Early Plays

Indeed, all these plays were a setting – out of the themes that would absorb me for a long time, as if I were beginning to discover what my subject would be. (*OAOP* p. xix)

Kureishi's early plays mark the debut of an instinctive, skilled dramatist and map the terrain of his subsequent work. In 'mirroring analytically' the complexity, fissures and diversity of the British Asian community and the racism (ranging from crude violence to more subtle, insidious forms) of sections of the white community, his dramas represent the emergence of his 'specular' role. Engaging almost immediately with Kureishi's major themes and conflicts, the plays explore the way immigrant experience is inflected by class, generation and gender and begin to debate the appropriate response to racism and the politics of representation. Kureishi's initial reception illuminates the socio-political contexts in which he began to write, and identifies the critical issues that were to dominate his career.

These plays are set in the late seventies in the context of high levels of inflation and unemployment that led to the hardening of the National Front movement which peaked in electoral terms in this era. National identity and national belonging were fraught issues. Margaret Thatcher's Conservative government, elected in 1979, marked a shift to the Right. Thatcher's speech justifying white British fears of being 'swamped' by 'people of other cultures' (made on television in 1978) is seen in retrospect as a crucial determining factor in her electoral success in 1979. This kind of xenophobia was translated in political terms into the flurry of anti-immigration legislation passed in the eighties.[1]

Kureishi's first two plays, *Tomorrow – Today!* and *The King and Me* are uncompromising portrayals of London's white underclass. *Tomorrow – Today!* is a snapshot of two bored and broke schoolboys who turn to crime. These characters are more developed in *Outskirts*. *The King and Me* depicts a married woman's obsession with Elvis Presley as a way of escaping the desolate monotony of her life. As the blurb of the first publication of his plays suggests, Kureishi was seen as a new voice that 'scours the urban wastelands for their discarded subjects and brings them screaming to life'.[2]

Nowadays the media describe Kureishi as a British writer. However, his early reception emphasized his outsider status. Early reviews categorize Kureishi as an 'Asian playwright' and emphatically *not* British: one explicitly contrasts his work with that of his British (read white) counterparts. His play *The King and Me* is described in *The Times* as 'another first-hand report from the bottom of the social heap. The difference is that, where British specialists in the field are apt to give their characters up for lost, Mr. Kureishi ends by showing that there are other escapes from the social trap than dreams.'[3] Here the difficulty of being (part) Asian and British is apparent. (Kureishi's mother's descent is frequently ignored.) Kureishi's skill in not allowing his outlook to be influenced by his 'Asianness' is praised! The same reviewer notes approvingly Kureishi's 'capacity to write about working class Britons [read white] without the least trace of ethnic bias' in *The King and Me*.[4]

Kureishi begins his exploration of racism and inter-racial dynamics in *Outskirts* and *Borderline*, first performed in 1981. The year in which African-Caribbean and Asian immigrants were defined as a problem, officially by the Conservative government's British Nationality Bill and Enoch Powell's calls for voluntary repatriation schemes for immigrant families in Britain. 'Unofficially', on the streets, black people were the victims of many racist attacks and murders, such as the firebombing of a party in New Cross that killed thirteen black youths in January 1981. The perpetrators were not found and the British establishment appeared unresponsive. It is within these socio-historical contexts that *Outskirts* – which revolves around a racist attack and the creation of a xenophobic fascist – needs to be examined.

Outskirts, first staged on 28 April 1981, won the George Devine award. Switching between two narratives, *Outskirts* explores the past and present of two white South Londoners Del and Bob. Kureishi handles the time-scheme and the vital transitions that have taken place in between expertly. His experimentation with time produces intense dramatic moments. He skilfully builds a dramatic tension from characters' shared guilty past. The occasion of the play is the protagonists' reunion when they revisit their violent assault of an Indian man twelve years ago. In retrospect the two men view the assault differently in relation to their respective 'development' as adults.

Bob now lives at home with his mother (who brought him up alone) and wife who despise him. Kureishi deploys these characters to evoke the domestic tensions of Bob's past and present in short, compressed but powerful scenes. The play's Pinteresque atmosphere of tension and menace derives from Bob's suppressed violence. He is unemployed, angry, depressed and a committed member of the National Front: an organization of 'strong men', 'ordinary...[s]olid English people' to whom he boasts about the attack. He insists that in the assault: 'We were cleaning something up. I understand that now' (*OAOP* 64–5). Del, on the other hand, has become an earnest, 'progressive' school-teacher: 'You know, what we did, years ago, you can't elevate it now' (*OAOP* 65). He calls Bob a fascist and now espouses a form of multiculturalism: 'There are...black children, in my class at school. Children of all colours. We learn about their cultures. The rest of the world can't be excluded. The rest of the world interests us' (*OAOP* 63). Del's spouting of multiculturalist rhetoric comes across as hollow. It is chilling to learn later that it was Del who got 'over-active' and had to be 'pulled...off the little Indian' by Bob (*OAOP* 74). At times, Del's shame over the assault appears to stem from a desire to protect his career. In this way, the audience's sympathies are not divided diagrammatically or schematically between the protagonists.

In his introduction, Kureishi locates Bob's fascism 'in the context of unemployment and nationalism of the late 1970s, and the despair they caused' (*OAOP*, p. xx). Bob insists 'This country, if anything, that's the ill one; not me' (*OAOP* 63). To an extent, the link between unemployment and fascism is maintained: the bleakness and stagnation of Bob's present life is powerfully conveyed and suggests why his viciousness became strengthened where Del's has dissipated: Del's teaching career has initiated his social mobility. He has moved beyond the 'outskirts'. However, what emerges from the play is that the brutal assault itself cannot be rationalized. The gratuitous violence of the act is clear. Del suggests that they attacked the Indian man because they were bored and 'wanted sensation' (*OAOP* 65). Bob's mother wistfully observes that in contrast to Bob, Del had 'brains and background' and 'attention' from his dad (*OAOP* 59). While this may have facilitated Del's move to the middle classes, it did not prevent him taking the initiative in the offence.

The scenes alternate between tense domestic interiors and the rubbish heap under the motorway, where the boys used to meet and where the attack took place: it is symbolic of urban wasteland and alienation. Reviewers comment on the opposition between *Outskirts'* grimly realistic setting and self-conscious dialogue. James Fenton criticizes 'the tension between anti-naturalistic writing and style of presentation'.[5] The *Guardian* review finds this very 'disjunction' between 'art dialogue in a tough setting' fascinating.[6] The dialogue produces an effect of defamiliarization. This disruption of a realist setting suggests a fractured, contingent society making the unified surfaces of realism impossible. As we will see, the breach between style and content will be a recurrent issue for Kureishi's critics.

There is some evidence that Kureishi's early play was favourably received by the white-dominated press, because of the compassion in his portrayals of the white attackers. *The Times* review of *Outskirts* suggests that as 'a British-born Pakistani who writes with some sympathy about the white urban working class, Hanif Kureishi is an inexpressibly welcome figure on the racial scene'. However, the reviewer goes on to discuss Bob's portrayal in a manner that verges on a rationalization of his racist behaviour that is not present in Kureishi's text. He refers to Bob's 'courageous independence ... he knows who he is. In a sense he rejected the system before the system threw him on the scrap heap'.[7] This suggests the way texts can be made to take on meanings by dominant critical views.

In this play, Kureishi focuses on the white attackers and their circumstances. These prototypes of British fascists remain with him: 'the boys from *Outskirts* were the genesis of the boys in *My*

Beautiful Laundrette' (*OAOP*, p. xx). In *Outskirts*, we never see the anonymous Indian victim, although we learn that to the boys' surprise he fought back. In his next play, *Borderline*, Kureishi begins to explore the other component in the equation, hitherto neglected in his work: forms of resistance to white racism. In *Borderline*, his British Asian subjects are not victims but activists.

BORDERLINE

In 1981, Max Stafford-Clarke of the Royal Court Theatre asked Kureishi to write and research a play for his Joint Stock Touring Company on the Asian immigrant community long established in Southall (a predominantly Asian area of West London). The result was *Borderline*. It opened on 2 November 1981, just months after a series of black uprisings had erupted in Toxteth, Southall and Brixton, forcing the British establishment to confront the extent of white racism and the degree to which black British people were alienated and marginalized. Kureishi's representations in *Borderline* are generated most specifically in the context of the Southall uprisings in 1979 when Asians opposed a provocative National Front pre-election rally, and in July 1981 when there were confrontations with both the National Front and the police.

Of all Kureishi's early plays, *Borderline* embodies most fully the themes he was to explore in his later work, while its multiple perspectives and generic hybridity became his characteristic mode. *Borderline* explores the different ways in which an immigrant family (Amjad, Banoo and their daughter Amina) has adapted to life in Britain. The play charts Amina's political radicalization, as she becomes increasingly involved in the Asian Youth Front led by Anwar and Yasmin. The youth movement's mobilization in response to growing attacks on Asians, their defiant response to racism, and their combative assertion that Britain is home and they are 'here to stay', are defined against their parents' reactions. The play closes with Yasmin reminding Amina 'We can't go home like your mother' and instructing her to keep the lights on in the Asian Youth Front Office so 'people know we are here' (*OAOP* 168). However, not all the young Asians agree on this approach: Amina adopts an activism that

25

her clandestine boyfriend Haroon rejects. Meanwhile, Anwar and Yasmin are initially hostile to a white journalist, Susan, who wants to join their fight against racist oppression. This antagonism refers to the debates on the role of white people in the collective struggles against racism of that era. The solidarity between African-Caribbeans, Asians and whites that characterized the anti-racist politics of the 1970s began to collapse by the 1980s: a decade of identity politics and debates on who is 'black' followed. In this play Kureishi disrupts notions of a monolithic Asian community by depicting one fractured by competing class interests. Kureishi counterpoints the alliances of the anti-racists with the way illegal immigrants are exploited as cheap labour by Haroon's father, a restaurateur who gives free meals to white policemen and displays notices condemning 'all those who plan any counter-demonstrations against neo-fascists' (*OAOP* 113).

Writing this play, Kureishi discovered the dramatic potential and the 'diversity' of the Asian community, largely by exploring its generational and gendered differences (*OAOP*, p. xix). *Borderline* deftly points to the various, complex factors that impinge upon immigrant experiences and the diverse responses to immigration. It presents a poignant portrait of first-generation immigrants rationalizing their decision to emigrate, weighing up the gains with the costs. The husband Amjad stresses the economic benefits that he as the male 'provider' has worked hard to secure for his family in Britain. He tells his wife Banoo that he does not want to return to Pakistan to 'be loved by your relatives' (*OAOP* 106). He implies that in Pakistan they would be dependent on Banoo's family. Banoo acknowledges their material gains but ruefully observes 'they haven't made us happy' (*OAOP* 127). She misses her family, her village and feels estranged from her daughter Amina who has become too 'English...grown so far from us...' and 'understands life here more than us' (*OAOP* 126–7). Banoo sees Amina's education in terms of a class mobility that exacerbates the distance between them: 'We are poor people. Where we come from, education is for the rich. But it has changed her and we can't understand' (*OAOP* 125).

The play highlights the gendered nature of some intergenerational conflicts. At first Amina finds ways to secretly elude the constraints her parents impose on her freedom, but by the end of the play she rejects the marriage arranged for her and symbolically cuts her long hair: a marker of 'traditional' South Asian femininity. Amina's internalization of these conflicts, manifested as a sense of guilt, is effectively delineated. Kureishi emphasizes the gap between parental expectations and reality by juxtaposing Amjad's attempts to police and obstruct Amina's sexuality and insistence that she is his 'baby girl', with scenes indicating her active sex life with her boyfriend Haroon. Her friend Yasmin prefigures the outspoken feminist anti-racist Jamila of *The Buddha of Suburbia*: 'for women like us, too much is dictated by other people. By our parents. And tonight by white racists (*OAOP* 167). We learn that Yasmin's father began to starve himself to death when she refused to accept an arranged marriage (*OAOP* 116). This is developed more fully as a subplot in *The Buddha of Suburbia*. Amina and Yasmin are the first in a series of Kureishi's British Asian female protagonists who find they cannot explore intellectual and sexual independence while remaining within the family. At the same time, Susan tells Amjad that her parents 'do mind' about her career as a journalist and that they 'think it's time [she] married an architect and had kids' (*OAOP* 127). This points to the gender constraints and patriarchal expectations in white British culture and prevents a simplistic contrast between a progressive white Britain and its 'backward' minorities.

Amina's family diverges in its response to their neighbours' racist attack on Amjad. Despite having suffered the racial assault, Amjad insists that a 'few' English racists should not force them to leave. He takes a court case against his aggressors, maintaining his belief in British democracy and the British legal system. In contrast, Banoo speaks of the failure of the police to uphold the law and protect them: 'the law wasn't there when the neighbour knocked you down...the police...said: go to hospital in a rickshaw' (*OAOP* 107). Kureishi's irony repeatedly foregrounds the discrepancy between vicious racial attacks and Britain's vaunted reputation as a liberal, tolerant society. For Banoo, living in fear of further racial hostility is unbearable: she wants to return to Pakistan, and does so after Amjad's death. For her daughter this is not an option: Amina says 'I belong here. There's work to be done. To make England habitable' (*OAOP* 158).

As Dick Hebdige reminds us, generational conflicts are produced in response to specific historical, cultural conditions and it is these contexts that need to be analysed to explain why these particular forms of discord should occur at a particular time.[8] Kureishi locates the Asian Youth Front's adoption of an alternative politics (to that of their parents) in terms of the militant protests against the escalating right-wing activities of the late 1970s. Avtar Brah observes that in the late 1970s, the media portrayed the Asian youth militancy as a new phenomenon and defined it in contrast to the political behaviour of their more 'docile' parents: this erased the history of the first generation's militant struggles in the 1950s, 1960s and early 1970s.[9] (Brah suggests the younger groups were not more 'progressive' than their elders, their resistance simply marked a new *form* of political agency, 'a home-grown British political discourse'.) In some ways Kureishi's work is in danger of reinforcing this discursive erasure, although Banoo's spirited response to her attackers prevents any easy, clear-cut generational divide: 'but I am not afraid. They do their things to us, but I will fight them' (*OAOP* 126). Moreover *Borderline*'s characterizations contest the media's effacing of the agency of female activists and exclusive focus on the role of black British males.[10] Kureishi explodes stereotypes of young British Asians as quiescent, passive, depoliticized, family types often defined in contrast to the more 'difficult' British African-Caribbean youth. An article in the *Sunday Telegraph* written in the aftermath of the Brixton riots in 1981 is an example of the way Asian youth were constructed as different from 'young blacks and some whites [who] have slipped completely from the control of their parents. Asians' culture has bound them tightly as both families and communities – in ways in which many white and black parents would envy'.[11] Kureishi's young Asian activists are endowed with a militant defiance that was considered the preserve of their African-Caribbean counterparts.

Kureishi's multigenerational focus delineates a community constantly evolving and redefining itself in response to changing cultural contexts, and so refutes static, reified representations. While Kureishi explores *inter*generational disagreements, he does not homogenize the divisions within each generation. A recurrent feature of Kureishi's writings is the way his British-born protagonists of Asian origin face and make a choice between competing ways of surviving in white Britain. The arguments for and against separatism and political activism form the central debate in *Borderline*, and resurface in *The Buddha of Suburbia* and *The Black Album*. While Haroon and the Asian Youth Front debate opposing political positions, *Borderline* hints at the more intangible tensions at the heart of Kureishi's work: the ambivalence and implications of solidarity to an 'ethnic' community and the competing demands of self and group.

Let's first look at the 'political' debate before turning to its more subtle concerns. Haroon explains why he chooses to pursue education rather than the separatist activism of the Asian Youth Front: 'We've got to engage in the political process. Not just put out fires when they start them. Yasmin and Anwar – they're brave. But they are separatist. I say we've got to get educated. Get educated and get inside things. The worm in the body...' (*OAOP* 118). Haroon articulates the argument that separatism reinforces boundaries between groups, and minorities remain at the socio-cultural margins of the body politic, while power remains within the homogeneous centre. Haroon desires instead to 'get inside things' and subvert them from within. Yasmin refutes Haroon's exhortation to abandon 'pointless' demonstrations and instead 'join parties, sit on committees' on the grounds of the inadequacy and 'slow progress' of 'existing machinery' while 'people are being burnt to death' (*OAP* 150). Yasmin counters Haroon's arguments, but in a manner characteristic of Kureishi, Haroon's points are not completely dismissed or negated. So while Yasmin feels it is 'crucial we defend ourselves', she contests those who 'imagine that all our work can be done with broken bottles and knives' (*OAOP* 164). As a leader of the youth movement, she tries to convey this to 'an office full of angry, ignorant boys' who 'talk of petrol bombs' and do not want 'to learn how to read and write' because they 'hate anything that takes longer than a night to achieve' (*OAOP* 141). On the eve of the demonstration, she agrees with Anwar that 'Tonight [protest is] the only possible response', but insists that she is 'already thinking about tomorrow' (*OAOP* 164). Yasmin's counter-argument asserts the importance of balancing confrontational activism (which involves both self-defence and retaliation) with a more proactive approach that will strengthen the community's status in the long term. In this way her stance is not so far from Haroon's. In this instance, Kureishi moves beyond a separatist/anti-separatist dichotomy in showing the relationship between the two positions as overlapping and complex.

The play closes with Yasmin's precarious attempt to prevent militant activism turning into gratuitous violence. Yasmin asks Amina not to take petrol to the riot: 'Retaliation is a necessity – sometimes. But some of us think it's a luxury. Put that back. There will be trouble tonight. Why add to it? It's us who have to sweep up in the morning' (*OAOP* 167–8). Yasmin's reiteration of the political impetus behind the 'riots' has important, topical implications in the context of the conflicting interpretations of the black uprisings. They represented either a fight for work and equality by alienated black British youth, or alternatively (to right-wing commentators) evidence of the hooliganism of criminal elements of black communities. Her observations are also an important acknowledgement of the range of different opinions within Asian communities. While Kureishi's sympathy for the activists is clear, this play also signals the anxiety about separatist activism that inflects all his writing. Yasmin, the 'responsible' rebel and moral centre of the play identifies positively with being British and suggests that mindless destruction only affects their community. Yasmin insists that she is not 'against things here. I want them to be improved' (*OAP* 167). Her position is one that a white liberal audience would find sympathetic. In an early interview, Kureishi positions himself as 'passing on life from people who really experience the rough end of things to people who might possibly be able to do something about that'.[12] However, it is clear that this play does not achieve the necessary dialogue with those who are far more alienated in Britain than Yasmin's portrayal suggests.[13]

Kureishi is not simply exploring the demerits and merits of separatist activism: he investigates the tensions and ambivalence of political commitment and group solidarity. First, solidarity is presented as difficult: it demands a self-sacrifice that Haroon resists. In contrast to the commitment of the militants, Haroon's refusal to engage with the activism of the Asian Youth Movement appears to be a rationalization of his personal ambitions to become a lawyer. Amina and the others perceive his individualism as a disloyal self-interest that prevails over his obligations to the community. At the same time, the suggestion that solidarity can be painful is treated sympathetically. Haroon demurs, partly because he does not wish to confront and adopt an embattled existence. For Amina (and the others) political engagement gives her a sense of belonging ('we were a community') and direction, Haroon plaintively observes, in contrast, 'I want to live a normal life...I suppose' (OAOP 149). For Haroon, distancing himself represents independence and freedom. Yasmin tells Haroon that his individualism is far from liberating because it stems from an internalization of 'race and contempt' as if 'it was some kind of personal problem you can work through on your own' which is ultimately self-destructive. She compares this to externalizing conflicts in the collective struggle against white racism, insisting: 'you can't live like that...It'll tear you apart in the end. No, we've got to organize and retaliate' (OAOP 149). Her description of Haroon echoes Kureishi's accounts of his childhood as marked by his sense that racism was a private problem.[14]

The oppressive aspects of solidarity to an 'ethnic' identity are not glossed over. Haroon feels 'cramped' and 'stifled' by the community 'Shut in for safety' (OAOP 117). For Haroon, this 'place and the past, it's like an octopus. You drag one limb off you while another's curled itself around you' (OAOP 100). As David Theo Goldberg observes, 'identity can also be a bondage within. It can keep people in who don't want to be in. And it can do so by insisting on an essential racial character, or simply by requiring racial solidarity.'[15] Haroon's stance is presented *both* as a self-centred evasion of commitment to the community (and to his girlfriend Amina) and equally as imperative for his self-development. Haroon is the first of a series of protagonists who can assert autonomy only by active detachment and 'leaving' the group. This articulation of conflicting perspectives (without obviously privileging one) is a characteristic feature of Kureishi's style, particularly the way he both ironizes and sympathizes with almost all his characters and refuses a final point of view. His ironic detachment becomes more pronounced later. Although even here the extent to which he is critiquing or naturalizing disengagement remains unclear.

As we will see in *The Buddha of Suburbia* and *The Black Album*, this tension between communal commitment and self-interest resurfaces, it is explored in this play in terms of the trajectory Anwar follows. Anwar and the white journalist Susan's ideological differences are suspended when they have a brief fling. When Anwar tries to extricate himself from her, it is in terms of the 'pleasure versus politics' polarity that Kureishi stages in *Sammy and Rosie Get Laid*, and *The Buddha of Suburbia* and which is most explicitly articulated in *The Black Album*. When Susan invites him over, Anwar declines, saying: 'Saturdays we patrol the area for trouble. What will they say if they find out I'm lying on a waterbed with a noseful of coke' (*OAOP* 150). In this play Anwar 'resists', but Kureishi's later protagonists are not so self-restrained.

Susan and Anwar's initial arguments extend the issue of separatism to engage with questions of representation: who controls the media representations of ethnic minorities? At first Anwar accuses Susan of appropriating the problems facing minority communities. His position begins as an essentialist one. He insists white people have no role in the struggle against unequal race-relations: 'White people are our problem and your Government in particular' (*OAOP* 134). Anwar's argument becomes more nuanced: he suggests that the dominant modes of representation of the white liberal press can distort and victimize the community:

> You change its nature as it passes through your hands. It drips pity. Somehow you say the right things. You talk about our 'problems'. You say we're victims.... The position you have – which reduces us. I suppose these things are always better coming from the patient than the nurse.... You take our voice. Replace it with your own. (*OAOP* 132)

Susan asserts that 'it's possible to be honest and accurate about other people's experience. I believe that's important, socially useful, if you like' (*OAOP* 132). She opposes the privileging of first-hand experience, insisting that there is no unmediated link between experience, analysis and ideological commitment: 'The fact that my life isn't lived out under threats and in fear doesn't mean I don't have integrity' (*OAOP* 133). Once again Kureishi juggles contradictory points of view, but perhaps the implication here is that while there are questions over privileged access to the media, political commitment is more important than cultural credentials. (This would be in keeping with Kureishi's contestation of the privileged insider.) In *Borderline*, conflicts over the representations of ethnic minorities occur between members of the dominant white majority and the oppressed minority communities. Kureishi's subsequent novel *The Buddha of Suburbia* reflects the way these arguments take place increasingly within the minority communities themselves. The debates between Susan and Anwar prefigure Karim and Tracey's dispute in *The Buddha of Suburbia*.

In *Borderline*, Kureishi finds a dramatic form of his own, weaving together elements of romance (with the secret meetings with between Haroon and the young Amina, outwitting her parents by sneaking out of the bedroom window) and realist and farcical comedy with a strong anti-racist, feminist perspective. This play is dotted with topical commentaries on race politics of the eighties that are not always well integrated. Its explicit, dialectical dialogue sometimes sounds like reportage from the frontline. For example, Yasmin declares, 'I think the Tories are working towards giving us only guest-worker status here. With no proper rights. That'll bring us into line with some EEC countries' (*OAOP* 115). In Kureishi's retrospective introduction, he critiques his efforts in *Borderline* to use 'a method, journalism, as the tool for a different form, art or theatre' (*OAOP* p. xix). He attempts to blend aesthetics and politics differently in his screenplays. Kureishi realized that his politics was not sufficiently embedded in his characters: 'I knew I had to find a way of knitting ideas to specific characters, events and emotions' (*OAOP*, p. xix). Haroon's father's capitalist ethic is more vividly and effectively actualized in Kureishi's portrayal of Nasser in *My Beautiful Laundrette*.

While the humour is not as sustained and developed in this play as it is in *My Beautiful Laundrette*, *Borderline* hints at his range. The theatre suits Kureishi's satiric spirit and he exploits opportunities for both dramatic and verbal irony and demonstrates his talent as a wordsmith. The withering sarcasm of his female protagonists, the quick-fire one-liners, the elements of *Carry on*-style slapstick, farcical comedy of mishap and mistaken identities, largely generated by Ravi (an illegal immigrant from

India whom Susan befriends), all blend in a way that will become distinctive of Kureishi's style: comedy pressed towards exuberant farce and the absurd. In both *My Beautiful Laundrette* and *Sammy and Rosie Get Laid* we see Kureishi's penchant for characters colliding with each other and falling over themselves. The farcical vein reflects the characters' confusion and dislocation. Equally characteristic is the way Kureishi sometimes resorts to generating humour by invoking facile stereotypes. Ravi is a clichéd figure of a sex-starved, randy Asian who arrives from India, imagining Britain as a sexual haven peopled with sexually available white women: 'You are English, please – undress!' ... 'I just wanted to touch your lovely round booblas' (*OAOP* 121). Ravi's portrait is so extreme it is tempting to see Kureishi underlining the artificiality of his own character here. This caricature is fleshed out into a fully developed character in Kureishi's Changez in *The Buddha of Suburbia*.

It is significant that *The Times* review singles out this hackneyed Asian character for praise and describes the scenes with the 'accident-prone Ravi' as 'simply the work of a fine dramatist with no axe to grind'. The same review describes Kureishi as 'the lone spokesman for the British Asian community'.[16] While Kureishi made the experiences of young British Asians more visible, this representation of Kureishi as the sole spokesperson is a white media construction. It ignores the polemical spokespersons for the black communities such as A. Sivanandan, as well as first-generation migrant writers who had already begun to explore the lives of young black Britons, such as Farrukh Dhondy in *Siege of Babylon* (1978), and *Come to Mecca and Other Stories* (1978).

Certain responses that surfaced in the reception of *Borderline* were to persist throughout his career: such as the pigeonholing of Kureishi as an 'ethnic writer'. Although his early portrayals of white working-class subjects received praise, reviewers clearly demarcate the representations of British Asians as Kureishi's area of expertise. James Fenton praises *Borderline*'s study of the Asian community in Britain as 'the best thing by Hanif Kureishi that I have seen'.[17] The *Times Literary Supplement* reviewer, while noting that his plays are about 'the suburbs rather than the subcontinent', suggests that it is as an 'Asian playwright, a voice from the ghetto that he has gained a reputation,' although the review concludes that *Borderline* makes clear that Kureishi is 'uneasy at being presented as a spokesman for the Asian community'.[18] Kureishi soon began to categorically resist the role of authentic insider or spokesperson foisted upon him. In his retrospective introduction to his early plays, he emphasizes his distance from this subject. He observes that 'research helped me to see the diversity and drama of the Asian community'. In relation to the other members of the Touring Company, he claims no extra insight into the community for himself: 'We knew the subject was there, but we couldn't get at it... not from the inside either: we didn't know enough' (*OAOP*, p. xix).

BIRDS OF PASSAGE

Kureishi's *Birds of Passage* (1983) is a more traditionally constructed and naturalist social drama. It is not as powerful as his previous plays. The play examines an Asian lodger's impact on a white suburban family. It anticipates *My Beautiful Laundrette* with its Pakistani protagonist Asif as a materially empowered agent, and in the way Kureishi does not flinch from showing his ruthlessness. Asif, a wealthy student, decides to buy the house of his white, unemployed working-class landlord David and his wife Audrey. He has a fling with Audrey's sister Eva and then discards her. Eva and Ted's disintegrating suburban marriage, beset with financial anxieties anticipates Ted and Jean's in *The Buddha of Suburbia*. The Chislehurst setting with its mixture of various forms of racism, bristling class tensions and aspirations would be more effectively realized in the novel form of *The Buddha of Suburbia*. Kureishi stopped writing plays because he 'stopped being able to find a tone or style to accommodate [his] voice or themes' (*OAOP*, p. xx). He finds this voice in the strong, detached ironizing first-person point of view of the novel's narrator Karim.

In *Birds of Passage*, Kureishi explores the intersection of race and class: the way race relations are inflected by class politics. Kureishi employs a strategy of anti-racist discourse, inversion to reverse the Manichean aesthetic of colonial discourse. Asif's remarks are rather self-consciously emblematic of the transposition of hierarchies: 'I'm going to be an expansionist... this house is the beginning of my empire' (*OAOP* 215). In contrast to Asif's entrepreneurial spirit, the landlord's children Paul and Stella are rootless and derailed. Stella becomes an upmarket sex-worker. This contrast between Asian immigrant success and the white working-class failure resurfaces in *My Beautiful Laundrette*. Not that class privilege always protects one from racism, as evidenced in the account of the reception Asif's father ('a high up' in Pakistan where 'no one can touch him') experienced in Britain: 'The last time he came here someone spat on him' (*OAOP* 185). A recurrent feature of Kureishi's characterizations of wealthy Asians is, as Gayatri Spivak describes, the migrant élite's 'comic yet ugly self-separation from the less advantaged of the former colony'.[19] Spivak is referring to Rafi in *Sammy and Rosie Get Laid*, but Changez in *The Buddha of Suburbia* makes similar snobbish observations on immigrants in Britain. Kureishi first articulates this tendency through Asif, who comments: 'Most English don't realize that the immigrants who come here are the scum of Pakistan: the sweepers, the peasants, the drivers... They've given us all a bad reputation here because they don't know how to behave (*OAOP* 200).

Set in the 1970s when unemployment and the resurgence of nationalism resulted in a construction of immigrants as a racial problem and as the determining factor in the present political crisis, this play examines the forms of racism articulated by the white suburbanites. For example, the parochialism in Ted's question to Asif: 'You're at one of our universities?' (*OAOP* 196). Ted's responses to Asif suggest how the positioning of whites as threatened second-class citizens allows racists to legitimize the exclusion of ethnic minorities. When Asif comments on the opportunities for Asians in Britain, Ted replies: 'That's true. Though I would put our people first' (*OAOP* 198).

In this play the argument over appropriate responses to racism takes a different form to that in *Borderline*: Asif and Paul debate whether vigilante activism or material empowerment is the most suitable weapon for combating racism. Here Paul takes on the activist role, joining Asian vigilante groups against the 'lumpen racists' (*OAOP* 215). He says: 'It's good to see them organizing and resisting' (*OAOP* 200). Asif mocks such militancy, insisting that 'There are other ways of achieving social peace. I've got some ideas. Prosperity is a great quietener, you know' (*OAOP* 200). Asif abandons his education, and decides to create a capitalist enterprise supported by his father's money. Asif dismisses Paul's involvement in the anti-racist movement: 'We don't need your help. We'll protect ourselves against boots with our brains. We won't be on the streets because we'll be in cars. We won't be throwing bricks because we'll be building houses with them. They won't abuse us in factories because we will own the factories and we'll sack people' (*OAOP* 215). That Asif's capitalist dream is accessible for only the privileged few is underlined in Paul's retort: 'Will everyone own factories or only those of you with wealthy fathers in Western-supported Fascist countries?' (*OAOP* 215). In *My Beautiful Laundrette*, the protagonist Omar rejects education (the path to empowerment outlined in *Borderline* by Haroon) in favour of Asif's capitalist ethic.

The Times review of *Birds of Passage* observes that Kureishi's characterization of the proud Asif differs from usual representations of Pakistani immigrants: 'It is . . . a salutary shock to see a Pakistani character elevated from *cornershop subservience* into the moneyed arrogance of an old Etonian'. The 'salutary' notwithstanding, his 'shock' reveals how deeply ingrained derogatory, narrow perceptions of Asian immigrants were (limited to the TV sitcoms such as *Mind Your Language*) and underlines the achievement of Kureishi's representations. Other critical issues emerged in his initial reception that would reappear, notably his ironic detachment. The same review of *Birds of Passage* compares Kureishi to Chekhov: 'if only because with Kureishi like Chekov you cannot tell where (if anywhere) the author's sympathies lie'.[20] The implications of Kureishi's ironic distance form the subject of the next chapter.

2

The Politics of Representation: Political Commitment and Ironic Distance

> I always want a bit of both with my characters: to send them up and to show them for real. That's the kind of comedy I like, when you can never make up your mind about things. (Kureishi, 1991)[1]

It was in the medium of film that Kureishi achieved his first major international success. Kureishi's screenplays of the 1980s, *My Beautiful Laundrette* (featured in Britain in 1985) and *Sammy and Rosie Get Laid* (released in 1988) about the culture of Thatcherism, mark a distinctive phase of his career with director Stephen Frears. Several reviews comment on the success of Frears's and Kureishi's collaboration: their shared interest in the complexities of culture and class and oblique approach to exploring the 'state of the nation'. Frears's eye for comic situation, the absurd, and his use of image for characterization make him a perfect foil for Kureishi's screenwriting. Frears's direction intensifies Kureishi's political concerns (the use of Thatcher's voice-over and the shots of derelict London) and contributes enormously to the braiding of surrealism and realism. The films are both a product and critique of the era. *My Beautiful Laundrette* (hereafter *Laundrette*) and *Sammy and Rosie Get Laid* (hereafter *Sammy and Rosie*) were literally products of the Thatcherite 1980s. Both were funded by Channel 4, a TV channel created in 1982, under Mrs Thatcher, with a brief to cater to minority representation. Kureishi both actively contributed to and benefited from this new space created in the media.

The creation of Channel 4 was partly in response to the controversial Scarman report into the uprisings of the early eighties. The Labour-controlled Greater London Council and other councils had already begun to acknowledge and promote ethnic and sexual minorities and their demand for representation, although the GLC was abolished by Thatcher in 1986. Kureishi observes the paradox: 'one plus of the repressive eighties has been a cultural interest in marginalized and excluded groups' (SRGL 63). At the same time, the spate and popularity, in the mid-eighties, of films about the British Raj – Forster's A Passage to India, Paul Scott's televised The Raj Quartet and M. M. Kaye's The Far Pavilions – were, as Rushdie observed, the 'artistic counterpart of the rise of conservative ideologies'.[2] Rushdie saw Thatcher's attempts to revivify notions of imperial glory in the Falklands war as excluding Britain's black populations, who felt differently about the empire. Kureishi suggests his rough, wild films on contemporary London were consciously formulated against both Raj revival 'lavish films in exotic settings' and genteel Merchant Ivory representations of Thatcherite heritage culture evoking an image of Englishness that encapsulated the identity only of its élite, ruling class (MBL 5). For Kureishi, the latter's recreations of England's past embody 'an effete quality that has nothing to do with the England I know, I mean England is horrible and full of drugs'.[3] Both Kureishi/Frears's films are rooted in the political and social climate of Thatcher's London. Laundrette delineates the empowerment of sections of London's Pakistani community able to prosper under Thatcherite enterprise culture.[4] Sammy and Rosie, often positioned as a more trenchant critique of Thatcherism, also evokes the disempowerment of the disparate elements of the British Left under the onslaught of nearly a decade of Thatcherism. Released in the year of Mrs Thatcher's third election victory, it needs to be examined in the context of the abolition of the GLC and the defeat of the trade unions and the miners' strike (1984–5).

Laundrette, rather than Kureishi's early plays, brought British Asian experiences and Kureishi into the wider public. It had a more far-reaching circulation than previous films about Asians in Britain, and was hugely successful, making the unexpected move into mainstream culture and commercial audiences.[5] Both his films met with controversy. Many of these responses can be examined in relation to a nexus of problems that constitute what Kobena Mercer summarizes as the 'burden of representation'. Namely, 'the assumption that minority artists speak for the entire community from which they come', which he argues both circumscribes the artist and reproduces the racist stereotype that 'every minority subject is, essentially, the same'.[6] The ways in which Kureishi's screenplays intervened in the debates on the 'burden' and 'politics' of black cultural representation will be the focus of this chapter.

Some responses highlight the commodification of black experience this wider publicity entailed. In a review of *Sammy and Rosie*, Pratibha Parma expresses her scepticism about the political impact of Kureishi's early films. She asks, 'does the commercialisation of black experience do anything to change it? And while we should be thankful that such films highlight and put black British experience on the international map, is this enough?'[7] In creating alternative black subjectivities, Kureishi's films clearly do more than put 'black British experience on the international map'. In contrast to Parma, in an influential essay in 1988, Stuart Hall interpreted Kureishi's screenplays (among others) as evidence of an important shift in black cultural politics. They mark the movement from black groups asserting their right to represent themselves and countering negative images with positive ones to a more complex agenda of a new 'politics of representation'. This new politics of black representation eschews positive images. It 'engages rather than suppresses *difference*' and thus entails 'the end of the essential black subject': the idea that a subject is constituted by 'authentic' fixed, pre-existent essences or characteristics. It registers instead 'the recognition of the extraordinary diversity of subjective positions, social experiences and cultural identities which compose the category "black"'. As we will see, the anti-realist elements of both Kureishi/Frears's films are an integral part of this 'new' politics of representation, formally foregrounding issues of representation and the impossibility of representing a stable external reality and fixed, coherent identities. With his complex, contradictory characters including gay Asian heroes, Asian and African-Caribbean feminists and lesbians, Kureishi not only explores a range of black identities, his intersections of ethnicity, gender, sexual orientation and class examine identity in terms of these multiple, overlapping and colliding categories. As Hall suggests, Kureishi's work illustrates that the question of the black subject cannot be represented without reference to these dimensions.[8] For Hall, this marks a divergence from 'a great deal of black politics, constructed . . . directly in relation to questions of race and ethnicity, [which] has been predicated on the assumption that the categories of gender and sexuality would stay the same and remain fixed and secured'.[9]

Hall observes that the shift in black cultural practice can be more accurately described as 'two phases of the same movement, which constantly overlap and interweave.'[10] This 'overlap' is embodied in *Laundrette* and to an extent in *Sammy and Rosie*. Kureishi's emphasis on the empowerment of his successful, ebullient Pakistani characters contests negative stereotypes of Asians as weak and oppressed. As Kureishi observes, none of his Asian characters are 'victims'.[11] At the same time, Kureishi does not substitute negative images for positive ones. His portrayals move beyond the positive or negative stereotypes dichotomy. This is a political move in terms of the politics of representation in offering 'new' black subjectivities. However, his films have provoked controversy and illustrate the difficulty of this move. It is not without risks: his ironizing and subversion of certain stereotypes makes him vulnerable to accusations of reinscribing others and underlines the precariousness of his position. The contradictory reception suggests the difficulty of reading Kureishi politically: his characterizations are read as pathbreaking or retrograde, even neo-orientalist. I would argue that his ironic distance is an integral component of his ambivalence and is at the centre of the problem of interpreting the politics of Kureishi's work. This is particularly evident in *Sammy and Rosie*.

MY BEAUTIFUL LAUNDRETTE (1985)

Laundrette describes the gay romance between Omar (Gordon Warnecke), a gauche but increasingly ambitious Anglo-Pakistani and his white former schoolmate Johnny (Daniel Day Lewis), an ex-National Front member. To the disgust of his gang, Johnny, sick of the violence, 'hanging around' and needing the money, agrees to help Omar refurbish a dilapidated London laundrette owned by Omar's entrepreneurial uncle Nasser (Saeed Jaffrey). Omar and Johnny become lovers. Omar finances the renovations by conning a sleazy relative, Salim (Derrick Branche), in a drug-trafficking deal. When Nasser virtually commands Omar to marry his daughter Tania (Rita Wolf), this causes a rift between Omar and Johnny, although they make up and commit a burglary to pay back Salim, who insists he only wanted to teach Omar a lesson not to 'bite the family hand' (*MBL* 59). Driving home, Salim deliberately knocks over and injures Moose, one of Johnny's gang. Meanwhile Tania decides to leave home disgusted by her father's affair with his white mistress Rachel (Shirley Anne Field) and stifled by her male-dominated family. The gang takes revenge for Moose's injuries by beating up Salim and smashing his car outside the laundrette. Johnny tries to stop the attack and is injured himself. Omar arrives, the gang disperses and the film ends with Omar bathing Johnny's injuries in the laundrette.

A synopsis cannot convey *Laundrette*'s lightness of touch that is the result of its pressing social issues and serious topics of racism set against the absurdity of its central project, the creation of the ritzy neon-lighted 'Powders' laundrette, complete with aquariums and hanging ferns. This combination is the film's most innovative feature and provides its controlling dynamic. Its social realist concerns commingle with gangster, thriller, comedy, fantasy and romance conventions. The gang's assault on Salim and Johnny is shot close up in brutal detail in keeping with the film's low-budget documentary realism. This is juxtaposed with the fantastic: a few frames earlier we see Rachel's blotched stomach disfigured by the magic potions created by Nasser's wife Bilquis, enraged by his infidelity. The film is also characterized by its non-realist, self-reflexive qualities: such as the one-way mirror in the laundrette, where we see two different 'illicit' relationships in ironic counterpart: Nasser dancing with his lover Rachel, and Omar and Johnny having sex in the back room. The closing image in the soaped-up laundrette is another example. Julian Henriques suggests, *Laundrette*'s break with realism expresses the 'feelings, contra-dictions and imagination of the characters' and the 'contra-dictory' nature of reality: '*Laundrette* spins round the multiple contradiction of a love affair between two men, two races and two politics' and 'the possibility of change'.[12] But Kureishi/ Frears's aesthetic is less a shift from realism than a mixture of realism and comic exaggeration.

42

The relationship between Omar and Johnny as they embark upon the laundrette project is at the centre of the film. Their intimacy defies both heterosexist norms and the communal policing that attempts to confine sexuality within ethnic boundaries. Both take considerable risks to be together, given the taboo of homosexuality, let alone inter-racial homosexuality, in their respective social contexts. The film underscores how sexual pleasure and desire complicate forms of cultural identification. In approaching the question of race through a male–male relationship, the inter-racial relationship is not solely examined as a white/black issue but is defined against the different forms of masculinity the film explores. For example, the heterosexist, patriarchal masculinity of Omar's family who cast aspersions on Omar's masculinity in phallic terms: Omar's father (Roshan Seth) asks Nasser to 'fix him with a nice girl. I'm not sure if his penis is in full working order (*MBL* 12). Similarly Nasser tries to pressure Omar to marry Tania with 'Your penis works, doesn't it' (*MBL* 46). Johnny's fascist gang's violent hyper-masculinity illustrates the ways in which a male culture of violence is a constitutive feature of racism. (Kureishi describes the area of south London where he was brought up, close to where Stephen Lawrence was killed, as 'very monocultural, very masculinist and rough'.[13]) The implication of *Laundrette* is that anti-racism becomes, in part at least, a gender issue and a question of redefining masculinity.

The inter-racial homosexuality is perceived by Gayatri Spivak as a 'didactic...solution to interracial problems'.[14] The *Times Literary Supplement* describes the film's last frame, with Johnny and Omar 'splashing each other with water over a sink', as portraying 'delightful individuals who, through love, have made a nonsense of racial antipathy'.[15] These interpretations simplify the film's complex treatment of this issue. While Omar and Johnny's sexual relationship is presented as a political site that is *potentially* liberating in transgressing race and class boundaries, it only gestures towards possibilities, and does not present any facile 'solution' to racism. Rather, the film emphasizes how issues of race and class configure personal relationships, closing not with a celebration of a lovemaking that transcends race, but with Omar bathing Johnny's wounds inflicted by racial conflict. The volatility of their contradictory and compelling relationship foregrounds its imbrication in wider societal conflicts. *Laundrette* captures the ambivalence, instability and precarious power dynamics in the master–slave relationship. Omar both wants to help Johnny and also needs him to renovate the laundrette. Their relationship is characterized by moments of eroticism, affection and humour; however, Omar feels a residual resentment of Johnny's previous appearances in neo-fascist marches against black people, particularly because of his father's attempts to help Johnny. Hence, Omar takes vengeful satisfaction in the fact that 'When we were at school, you and your lot kicked me all around the place. And what are you doing now? Washing my floor. That's how I like it. Get to work I said. Or you're fired' (*MBL* 51). Johnny wants to expiate his earlier involvement with the racist skinheads: 'Nothing I can say, to make it up to you. There's only things I can do to show that I am . . . with you (*MBL* 44).

The power dynamics of Omar and Johnny's relationship need to be measured against the backdrop of the empowerment of this group of Pakistanis and the disempowerment of sections of the white working class. The film tackles the race and class tensions between Johnny's former white street gang and Omar's family. In contrast to the white unemployed youth, Omar's uncle Nasser understands and embraces Thatcherite enterprise culture and is able to prosper in it. In the face of the embourgeoisement of this section of the Asian community, the gang vent their frustrations in racist verbal abuse and attacks. White resentment of the reversal of white/black power relations is symptomatic of and fuels racism in *Laundrette*, set in the context of unemployment and nationalism of the 1980s. Genghis, one of the white street gang feels both infuriated and insecure when he sees Johnny, a white boy, work for an upwardly mobile British Asian, Omar: 'I don't like to see one of our men grovelling to Pakis. They came here to work for us. That's why we brought them over. OK?' (*MBL* 38). 'Grovelling' suggests an appeal to the masculinist culture of the gang in wanting Johnny to stop this demeaning behaviour. '*We* brought them over' is a desperate attempt to reinstate control, as well as denying agency to and dehumanizing the imported people, and suggests how ideas of masculinity are shaped in relation to ideologies of race *and class.*

The film depicts the sullen, alienated white 'tormentors' on the street, evicted by their 'victims' who themselves live in luxury homes. Perminder Dhillon-Kashyap suggests this distorts the perspective on race politics and exculpates the white fascists:

> the film has created a new victim, the white fascist – a victim of economic circumstances – who is being exploited by petty bourgeois Asian businessmen. Consider the opening scene of the film – two white fascists have been thrown out by black heavies on the orders of Salim (Derrick Branche). Instantly, the film attempts to engage the spectator's sympathy towards these fascists.[16]

Certainly, Kureishi does not shy from criticizing Nasser and Salim's merciless tactics as slum landlords: they embody the ruthlessness of the Thatcherite ethos of competitive individualism and the erosion of social responsibility. Part of Kureishi's critique of Thatcherite culture is that the working class (including ethnic minorities) has been disenfranchized by her policies. Dhillon-Kashyap's response shows the difficulty of thematizing this point without being interpreted as 'justifying' racism.

In his portrayals of Nasser and Salim as 'too busy keeping this damn country in the black. Someone's got to do it', Kureishi subverts racist stereotypes of Asian immigrants as a drain on the country's resources by 'sponging off' the state (*MBL* 14–15). In fact their unscrupulous enterprise creates employment for the white unemployed and is an ironic interpretation of Thatcherite policy. Robert Stam and Ella Shohat argue that the film departs from 'realist' models productively to create 'a provocative symbolic inversion of conventional expectations of a miserabilist account of Asian victimization'.[17] The text self-consciously asserts psychological as well as material empowerment. The Pakistani characters have a robust assertiveness and confidence. In 'The Rainbow Sign', Kureishi counters racist predictions that 'mixed-race' children will form a lost generation of 'misfits' in Britain. (Second-generation children were similarly constructed.) Kureishi characteristically points out the clash between his own subjective experiences and this form of 'victimization' which he suggests was a societal projection of its own ambivalence (*MBL* 75). This subversion of pathological constructions of mixed-race children 'caught between two cultures' is dramatized in *Laundrette*. To the white youth, Omar is a 'wog boy', to Salim he has 'too much white blood' and he is patronized by Cherry (ironically an Anglo-Indian herself) as an 'in-between' (*MBL* 29, 20, 28). Omar remains unconcerned by these projections that are not his problem. He is consumed by his relationship with Johnny and intent only on how to make it in Britain. This refusal of victimization is paralleled in the way the boys' homosexuality is 'taken for granted'. Kureishi wanted to make a film that did not end with one or other of the gay couple 'killing themselves'.[18] This was an important positive assertion in the mid-eighties when, at the height of the AIDS panic, with the media linking AIDS to homosexuality, Britain was at its most homophobic.

While Kureishi contests certain negative stereotypes, he creates not positive but contrary Asian characters with both shortcomings and strengths. This is best illustrated in the portrayal of Nasser. In a manner suited to the transient, immediate film medium, Kureishi distils Nasser's character in a few memorable sentences: Nasser's advice to Omar to learn how to 'squeeze the tits of the system' embodies both his capitalist ethic and callous sexism (*MBL* 17). Nasser is portrayed as an exploitative, venal, passionate man. Yet despite the critique of his ruthless ethos and patriarchal double standards, the high-living Nasser is an attractive character with an exuberant passion for Rachel and a genuine love and desire to help his brother and nephew.

When *Laundrette* was released, several Asian critics focused not on Kureishi's subversion of pernicious stereotypes, but on his reinforcement of them. Mahmood Jamal claims Kureishi reinscribes dominant perceptions of Asians as 'money-grabbing, scheming, sex-crazed people'.[19] The realist assumptions taken for granted in Jamal's critical framework underline the extent to which the burden of representation assumes and privileges realism. The realist aesthetic serves to reinforce 'the tokenist idea that a single film can be regarded as "representative" of every black person's perception of reality' and the assumption that 'reality has an objective existence "out there," that the process of representation simply aims to correct'.[20] Jamal's criticisms are caught up in what Shohat and Stam identify in *Unthinking Eurocentrism* as 'the moralistic and essentialist traps embedded in a "negative-stereotypes" and "positive-images" analysis.' This is precisely the trap that Kureishi wants to break from. Shohat and Stam suggest a methodological alternative to an analysis grounded in examining mimetic positive images or hostile distortions. Such an approach would pay less attention to the film's accuracy to sociological truths and focus instead on its articulation of the range and interplay of voices and perspectives of the community or communities in question. A more 'nuanced' critical approach would examine 'the cultural voices at play, not only those heard in aural "close-up" but also those distorted or drowned out by the text. ... to "bring out" the voices that remain latent or displaced'.[21]

With this critical framework in mind, we can see that Kureishi gives voice to the diverse perspectives of the community. Kureishi does not homogenize the experiences of first-generation migrants: they are not all 'money-grabbing'. Omar's left-wing father and the Asian poet whom Nasser evicts illustrate that not all Asians have prospered from the enterprise culture, nor support it. In fact a characteristic feature of Kureishi's work is its articulation of a range of conflicting voices. Omar's father wants him to leave the laundrette and return to college, insisting that education is power and that Omar 'must have knowledge. We all must, now. In order to see clearly what's being done and to whom in this country' (*MBL* 53). However, this voice is 'drowned out' by the narrative. Omar's father's decline into poverty enhances the appeal of his uncle's ethic that money is the source of power and mobility, rather than education. Nasser asserts his identity in relation to class and not race and negates the power of racism in the face of capitalist success. He insists 'I'm a professional businessman not a professional Pakistani. There's no such thing as race in the new enterprise culture' (*MBL* 41). Salim observes the converse aspect of this perspective, in ruefully commenting on Omar's father's decline from Bhutto's close friend in Pakistan to bedridden, impoverished socialist in Britain: 'But we're nothing in England without money' (*MBL* 48). While certain stances are structurally privileged, all are subjected to scrutiny and interrogated. Kureishi maintains an ironic distance, posing difficult questions and resolutely refusing to provide closure. He gestures towards a range of possibilities from which the reader/viewer can develop his/her opinion.

47

Tania provides a critique of her father's business ethic, but she is structurally marginalized in this narrative of the two male buddies. Inderpal Grewal argues that in *Laundrette* Kureishi 'does not do too well with feminist issues. The hero's cousin, a young girl who rejects the accepted role of women in both the English and Pakistani cultures, ultimately cannot be accommodated in the film. She disappears at a railway station, and this disappearance seems to be the only *solution* for a feminist Asian woman'.[22] Grewal's response points to the expectations of critics who seek overt political solutions especially perhaps in a text authored by a minority artist. Perhaps Kureishi suggests leaving home may be the 'solution', which underlines the way he gives you politics but not in a way you might want or expect. At one level, Tania's running away follows a clichéd trajectory, although it can be argued that here Kureishi depicts the way some British Asian women are faced with such stark choices. At the same time, responses such as Grewal's register an implicit disappointment that Kureishi fails to promote change or present alternative possibilities for circumventing cultural and sexual positioning.[23] What Tania's disappearance makes clear is the way the film (and this is true of Kureishi's work in general) is not centrally interested in the women characters or what happens to them. While Kureishi skilfully delineates complex, realistic Asian and western female protagonists and takes pains to empower them, often giving them the sharpest lines, they function primarily as foils to the men. His work is chiefly concerned with masculinity.[24]

In his characterization of Tania as fearless, outspoken and sexually free, Kureishi contests the trope of the submissive Asian daughter and undermines stereotypes of Asian women as passive and desexualized. However, the episode where Tania bares her breasts through the window has troubling implications from a feminist perspective. From the point of view of the narrative, this act is positioned as a deliberate, transgressive act against patriarchal norms and expectations of women. Kureishi has described this scene as Tania's chance 'to be liberated for a few moments'.[25] But, this interpretation derives from a problematic notion of politicized femininity or political consciousness and as Dhillon-Kashyap argues Tania's act positions her literally in the 'voyeuristic gaze' of white male fantasies of the sexually exotic other. Rita Wolf (who played Tania) rejects Kureishi's interpretation of this event and describes the impact of the experience from the point of view of an actress. She suggests the 'lasting effect this particular incident seemed to have on critics and public alike, coupled with the fact that it is the best film role I have been offered to date, suggests how little things have changed'.[26] As Wolf implies, the exclusive focus on this aspect of Tania's nonconformity diminishes her wider critiques of sexism. The characterization of Tania exemplifies the difficulty of reading Kureishi's politics. In some instances it stems from (as we saw with Grewal) his refusal to provide a clear political message or the positive 'solution' we may want, and at other times, his portrayals are problematic in themselves, marked by patriarchal flaws.

Kureishi appears to have accurately anticipated the hostility he would face with *Laundrette*:

> I don't know how the Asian community will deal with it: they think that I'm perpetually throwing shit at them anyway. They'll think that this is the last straw: now he's showing us as drug dealers, sodomites and mad landlords. But then I don't pretend to be a spokesman for the Asian community, and they shouldn't expect me to do PR for them, any more than you'd expect Neil Jordan to do PR for the Irish community...[27]

Kureishi justifiably refuses to take on the role of representing 'the Asian community'. More recently he suggests that being 'so diverse, so broad in terms of class, age and outlook... it doesn't make sense to talk about the so-called Asian community'. He observes, 'the importance of having a full range of writers writing about this community is precisely because of this rich disparity'.[28] He comments: 'If I want to show an Asian junkie, then I'll show an Asian junkie. Or an Asian heroin dealer. *But I know that I'm not saying that all Asians are heroin dealers because it is not true.* I might write about a heroin dealer because it might be interesting to me'.[29] However, while his portrayals are not intended as representative, we need to distinguish this from their political *effect*. The negative stereotypes could provide a safe outlet (safe because articulated by Kureishi, one of 'them') for the fears and prejudices of some of the dominant viewership.[30] This is the crux of Jamal's objection to *Laundrette*. His suggestion that the film was popular with European audiences because 'it says everything they thought about us but were afraid to say' cannot be dismissed as a knee-jerk reaction to unflattering portraits of his community. Jamal is concerned with the implications of the release of these representations into a context where they can be manipulated by racists. His objections to the film are specifically located in the context of years of minimal, overwhelmingly negative representation of ethnic minorities: 'Being constantly misrepresented in the media can make one unbearably sensitive to issues of stereotyping and lead us into protecting and defending every stain that shows up when we wear our badly washed clothes'.[31]

As Judith Williamson suggests, 'The more power any group has to create and wield representations, the less it is required to *be* representative.'[32] *Laundrette* appeared when there was not 'the full range of writers' to represent the community's variety. The paucity of representation was far greater than it is today. Early reviews of *Laundrette* emphasize the novelty of this portrait of London's Pakistani community and provide insights into the context within which the film was received. Frears claims, before *Laundrette* 'Nobody had any idea that this world existed'.[33] The *New York Times* suggests '*My Beautiful Laundrette* opened the *surprising, hitherto obscure* world of London's Indian and Pakistani immigrant cultures to public scrutiny'.[34] Another review describes it as 'a film that *seemed to come out of nowhere*, a splattered cinematic canvas'.[35] Although the less popularized works of Farrukh Dhondy and Tariq Mehmood are ignored in these white media constructions of Kureishi, this *perception* of Kureishi as the first and only writer to depict the British Pakistani community gives his work a representative status.[36] As Isaac Julien and Kobena Mercer suggest, 'if only *one* voice is given the "right to speak", that voice will be heard, by the majority culture as "speaking for" the *many* who are excluded or marginalized from access to the means of representation'.[37]

Consider also, Frears's comments on *Laundrette*: 'It was astonishing because [Kureishi] got it so right. That someone could be so right, so confident about it, make the jokes, be so on the inside.'[38] How can Frears, or anyone else, confer this authenticity? This raises the questions: whose representations of ethnic minorities are represented and received? Who controls them? Who authorizes them? As Sneja Gnew observes, 'the whole *notion* of authenticity... is one that comes to us constructed by hegemonic voices'.[39] Certain authors who address the dominant culture are privileged over others. Uma Narayan suggests that the privileging of these preferred insiders allow the majority community to refrain from criticizing the minority, because the function of providing a critical or dominant liberal perspective on the Other culture is assigned to the 'Authentic insider.'[40]

The responses to *Laundrette* dramatize the way minority artists and critics appear to be divided into two camps. On the one hand, critics such as Jamal and, implicitly, Perminder Dhillon-Kashyap perceive the role of the minority artist as necessarily didactic, in order to reduce 'the imbalance caused by decades of misrepresentation and stereotyping... [in] the media in general'.[41] On the other hand, critics such as Stuart Hall assert the importance of films like *Laundrette* and *Sammy and Rosie* lies in their very 'refusal to represent... black experience in Britain as monolithic, self-contained, sexually stabilized and always "right-on" – in a word, always and only "positive"'.[42] In defence of Kureishi's films (and his own work), Rushdie observes: 'the real gift we can offer our communities is not the creation of a set of stereotyped positive images to counteract negative ones, but simply the gift of treating black and Asian characters, in a way that white writers seem rarely able to do... as fully realized human beings, as complex creations, good, bad'.[43] Finally, although Jamal and Dhillon-Kashyap raise legitimate questions concerning the political impact of Kureishi's portrayals, to follow their arguments to their logical conclusion would be to constrain the minority artist into replacing negative portrayals with positive ones and 'to be kept captive by the racist prejudices of the majority'.[44] This would result in images of minorities circumscribed by a few narrow stereotypes, without any degree of heterogeneity and complexity. So I would agree with Hall and the others. Kureishi's artistic response to the diversity and complexity of British Asian experiences is a progressive deconstruction of received, conventional assumptions of minority communities and leads to a broader self-definition. However, although Kureishi ironizes certain stereotypes, because his critique of, for example, fat cat Asian businessmen feeds into negative stereotypes of Asians, his subversion and reinforcement of stereotypes appear inextricably entwined. This underscores the precariousness implicit in trying to move beyond positive/negative binary. *Laundrette* is characterized by an ironic distance, a setting up of possibilities, but a refusal to privilege or provide answers. As we will see this ambivalence and ironic distance are even more pronounced in *Sammy and Rosie.*

SAMMY AND ROSIE GET LAID 1988

Kureishi's second, more stylized, screenplay, also directed by Frears, was funded by the American company Cinecom and Channel 4 and made on a $2 million budget. It met a mixed critical reception. This film revolves around an increasingly unsatisfying 'open' relationship between British Asian Sammy, a self-indulgent, immature accountant (Ayub Khan Din), and Rosie (Frances Barber), a hip, white, feminist social worker. Sammy is jealous of Rosie's lovers, even though he is sleeping with an American photographer (Wendy Gazelle) who is preparing an exhibition called 'Images of a Decaying Europe'. Rosie begins an affair with Danny (Roland Gift), a gentle, enigmatic British African-Caribbean squatter. Danny provides a connection to the commune: a multi-ethnic band of musicians who surreally drift through the streets playing music, and camp in a wasteland under a motorway. The squatters and their commune become the focal point of critique of Thatcher's erosion of the welfare state and cuts in public spending and neglect of the poor, the displaced and the unemployed. Danny also forms a link to sections of the black community who riot in protest at the shooting of a black woman in a police raid, at the start of the film. This is loosely based on the actual accidental shooting of a British African-Caribbean woman, Dorothy 'Cherry' Groce, in a police raid on her home where her son was sought in 1985. (In actuality this shooting was followed one week later by the death of another British African-Caribbean woman Cynthia Jarrett, who died of a heart attack during a police raid on her house provoking the uprisings at the Broadwater Farm estate.)

Sammy's father Rafi (superbly played by Shashi Kapoor) is the catalyst of the story. An affluent factory owner and brutal politician (from, presumably, Pakistan), Rafi has returned to his 'beloved' London after a thirty-year absence to find the streets aflame with tumultuous riots and looting. He has come to be reunited with the son he abandoned and give him his inheritance, see an old flame he also deserted, Alice (Claire Bloom), a romantic yet commonsensical bourgeois English woman, and to protect his life, which he fears is in danger. Rafi is a complex figure: charismatic, sympathetic, hedonistic and sexist. Gradually his complicity in sanctioning tortures to maintain a fascist regime in his homeland is unearthed by the inquiries of Rosie's friends. Rafi's discussions with Alice and his encounter with the commune remind him of the disintegration of his previously 'liberal' views. As Colin MacCabe suggests the weight of the film's historical past is the effects of colonial history and the 'regimes that were established by national liberation struggles' in the subcontinent.[45] The surreal ghostly figure of the tortured Asian taxi-driver with one bandaged eye haunts Rafi, forcing him to confront the cruelties he authorized to sustain a repressive dictatorship: his desecration of 'all human life' (SRGL 53). The film closes with Rafi's suicide, hinting at Sammy and Rosie's *rapprochement*.

Sammy and Rosie lacks the controlling dynamic of the earlier film's laundrette project and is therefore weaker. The film's rapid cross-cutting between multiple storylines and the portrayal of six lives in counterpoint against the backdrop of a turbulent London results in an unfocused, fragmented narrative. At the same time, the formal disruptions of the filmic text (the parallel editing, voice-overs, swish pans, and elements of farce) fracture conventions of naturalism and give expression to the social contradictions and turmoil of Kureishi's London. The cross-cutting between characters de-emphasizes continuous narrative and a single point of view, suggesting multiple perspectives, social contexts and the intersection of disparate lives. This is most noticeable in the sequence of images depicting the intertwining lives and couplings of the main characters, culminating with a split screen where we are presented with the three central couples having sex in different places. *Sammy and Rosie* also lacks a central relationship as interesting and compelling as that of *Laundrette*. Sammy is a flat, spectral figure upstaged by both Rosie and Rafi. The characters take on a somewhat emblematic function and articulate their politics in self-consciously literate, witty sometimes glib dialogue.

In terms of his specular role, Kureishi's movement from *Laundrette* to *Sammy and Rosie* charts his shift from an illustration of sections of London's Pakistani community, to a more diverse cross-section of South Londoners. Namely, British African-Caribbeans, whites and Asians, middle-class liberals and the homeless and dispossessed of Thatcher's London. *Sammy and Rosie* marks Kureishi's increasing interest in class, politics, sex and relationships. Kureishi has no desire to make a minority or ghetto film, and has emphasized the limitations of such an approach:

> What we need is imaginative writing that gives us a sense of the shifts and difficulties within a whole society. If contemporary writing which emerges from oppressed groups ignores the central concerns and major conflicts of the larger society, it will automatically designate itself as minor, as a sub-genre. And it must not allow itself to be rendered invisible and marginalized in this way.[46]

Accordingly the second film pays more attention to the social inequity of Thatcher's Britain. Frears describes *Sammy and Rosie* as 'a much bleaker film, but then the times were worse' in contrast to the 'cheerfully defiant' *Laundrette*.[47] The most strident feature of *Sammy and Rosie* is its pointed critique of Thatcher's policies. The pre-credit long shot of the wasteland accompanied by Thatcher's smug voice-over, declaiming 'we have got a lot of work to do in some of our inner cities' cues the viewer to the film's political content. The squatters are bulldozed off their camp in this wasteland by property developers encouraged by the government; censure of the brutal policing of black communities is expressed in the murder at the start of the film. The government's repressive sexual morality and homophobia is contested by the emphasis on sexual pleasure and critique of heterosexism. But *Sammy and Rosie* also dramatizes the disempowerment of the 'demoralized, disorganized and disaggregated' elements and factions of the British Left in the eighties and its repeated failure to create an effective opposition to Thatcherism.[48] The film was released after Mrs Thatcher's third re-election to power, with Labour reeling from the magnitude of its defeat, which Kureishi (a member of the Labour party) documents in his diary that accompanies the screenplay.

This disempowerment is illustrated by the liberated but directionless, central couple, the aimless black British 'revolutionary' and the ambiguity of the eviction scene juxtaposed against the backdrop of London in crisis. A striking feature of *Sammy and Rosie* is that it is steeped in political upheaval and yet the protagonists are all characterized by a political paralysis. bell hooks's seminal essay on *Sammy and Rosie* illuminates the ambivalence of its treatment of issues of race and resistance and attributes this ambivalence as symptomatic of Kureishi's 'stylish nihilism'.[49] While Kureishi's work incrementally appears to privilege disengagement, I would argue that the ambivalence hooks elucidates in the film is a product of Kureishi's attempts to thematize or illustrate the failures of resistance. What both the film itself and responses to the film confirm is that the difficulty of interpreting Kureishi politically stems from his ironic distance.

Let's begin with a discussion of the ways in which *Sammy and Rosie* reveals the ambivalence operating on Kureishi's treatment of race and resistance to racial oppression. As hooks suggests, the film's opening scene, where the black woman is shown slinging the hot oil in which she is frying chips at the policeman, suggests that the police are responding to a perceived threat and this blunts the sharp edge of minority politics. The political implications at stake become clear when we consider that in contrast to Kureishi/Frears's fictionalized narrative, Channel 4 refused to transmit Ceddo's *The People's Account* because it objected to the description of Mrs Groce as 'a victim of police racism'.[50] So although, as Spivak suggests, Channel 4's support of Kureishi/Frears's films indicates its desire to educate the 'dominant viewership about the minorities', it also privileges work that this dominant viewership will find acceptable and sympathetic.[51] This is what Kureishi/Frears provide despite their (self-)construction as controversial anti-establishment figures making films 'shrieking' at Mrs Thatcher.

Although the shooting illustrates the impetus behind the uprisings, the protest itself descends into a performance: with black looters posing for their photographs to be taken in the midst of the riot foregrounding the film's departure from realist accounts. This points to a contradiction operating in Kureishi's work: it is at one level steeped in racial issues, and at the same time this focus on race is undermined by an ironic disengagement. Despite the violent social context of race riots and police brutality in *Sammy and Rosie*, the issues of race and racism are not explored in any depth. In *Sammy and Rosie* the shooting incites the rebellion, confrontation and violence that provide the backdrop of the film and remain in the background. We learn that the woman who was killed acted as a foster mother to Danny. Danny's politics are not developed beyond his reference to Gandhian nonviolence and domestic colonialism in Britain. Danny observes the uprisings from the sidelines. Echoing Yasmin from *Borderline*, he fears 'if full-scale civil war breaks out we can only lose' and sentimentally expounds, 'And what's going to happen to all that beauty' (*SRGL* 21). The grave dilemma he faces over how to respond to the murder of 'an old woman [he] loved' is articulated, but not examined. He rejects violence but at the same time wonders if he 'should be doing it' (*SRGL* 51).[52] hooks cites a young black male viewer whose 'identification with the character of Danny reinforced the sense of powerlessness'.[53] It seems to me that Kureishi is thematizing this sense of powerlessness as a problem, articulating the directionlessness of a black person who wants to find other modes of protest, when no political avenues are open to him. In 'The Rainbow Sign', Kureishi attacks the Labour party's refusal to confront the racism of some of its supporters and keenly observes, 'if the Labour Party occasionally wishes blacks to serve it, it does not desire to serve blacks' (*MBL* 96). Danny's powerlessness is both a product and symptom of the decline of the Left.

hooks further observes that Danny is 'totally distracted by his sexual desire for Rosie' and argues that all the male characters 'use sexuality as a way to escape their inability to respond politically'.[54] Again this is not a slippage, as hooks seems to imply, the film thematizes the way sexual pleasure obscures political commitment. This points to another area of ambivalence that is key to Kureishi's work in general. As I have argued, sex is politicized but at the same time it is in tension with forms of political commitment and action. The explicit emphasis on sexual pleasure bears a complex relationship to other forms of politics articulated in this film. On one hand, the most transgressive impact of the film is its contestation of the Conservative, heterosexist ethos of Thatcher's government represented in the values of Rafi and Alice's generation.[55] Rafi and Alice collude in their heterosexism describing Rani and Vivia respectively as 'perverted half-sexed lesbians' and 'odious and unnatural' (*SRGL* 46, 43). The lesbians' witty description of heterosex is one of the ways in which the film satirizes heterosexism: 'that stuff when the woman spends the whole time trying to come, but can't. And the man spends the whole time trying to stop himself coming, but can't' (*SRGL* 33). Similarly, the famous sequence with three pairs of adulterous lovers having sex (sarcastically set to Motown's 'My Girl' and playing on dissonance) is an affirmation of sexual pleasure in response to Thatcher's call for a return to Victorian values. Kureishi defines this resurgence as the 'mean monogamous spirit of our age': a repressive morality and agenda for the eighties read as a backlash against the excesses of the sixties (*SRGL* 118).[56]

On the other hand, sex usurps the centre stage of this filmic text eclipsing the incendiary racial conflict and squatters' protests. All the protagonists (not only the men) are governed by sex. This is the direction of the narrative. The text privileges sexual pleasure, structurally and visually. The horizontally split scene or (as Kureishi describes it) the 'fuck sandwich' forms the centre and climax of the film: 'I wrote around it.'[57] The rest of the film deals with the reverberations of these sexual acts. Kureishi originally wanted to call the film 'The Fuck'. He notes that the eviction scene was added only subsequently (*SRGL* 70). This is how it appears in the film. In contrast to *Laundrette*, where inter-racial homosex is about resisting ethnic and gendered stereotypes, forming a transgressive bond against dominant society and destabilizing notions of community based on ethnicity, in *Sammy and Rosie* the subversive potential of sex is more limited. Casual sexual liaisons in the context of the murder of a black woman are not so much liberating as escapist.

Just as the black uprisings are portrayed ambivalently, the squatters' resistance to the property developers is treated ambiguously: it is shown as positive but ultimately ineffectual.

Deliberately evocative of the sixties communes, the wasteland represents Kureishi/Frears's homage to the ideals of that age. The commune with its flames, ballerinas, metal sculptures, intricate chess sets and T. S. Eliot's *The Waste Land* painted on the caravan is deliberately romanticized and utopian. (It is more sentimentalized than the black rioters.) Kureishi/Frears conceived the squatters' protests as a celebration of young people's 'vivacity, lack of conformity and rebelliousness' (*SRGL* 103). During the eviction, the squatters *'remain defiant, cheerful and rebellious, like the PLO leaving Beirut* (*SRGL* 56). Yet ultimately they fail. The eviction is a warning to show 'how illiberal and heartless this country has become' and implies that the sixties opposition tactics are ultimately ineffectual in the context of the eighties (*SRGL* 56). Kureishi/Frears's interest is confined to thematizing the problem of resistance rather than exploring political repercussions and alternatives.

Frears describes *Sammy and Rosie* as 'an attempt to bring Mrs Thatcher down. It clearly failed. It's actually very overt in its attempts to rally the troops.'[58] The film is pointed in its critique of Thatcher, but, as we have seen, 'the troops' are not spared Kureishi's satire. To a greater extent than *Laundrette*, *Sammy and Rosie* is marked by Kureishi's pervasive ironic, detached style. Many reviewers praise the way *Sammy and Rosie* eschews political didacticism and dogmatism, and embraces irony, ambiguousness and contradiction. Leonard Quart observes that while 'the film's prime sympathies lie with the deviant and the disorderly...Kureishi and Frears are too subtle to turn their sympathies into some Manichean vision of the virtuous hip and the repellent straight'. Quart valorizes the way that the 'radical elements – ranging from the two lesbian women to the rioters' – are 'treated with unpredictable irony and bite'.[59]

However, as other responses to Kureishi suggest, the 'burden of representation' also demands a level of engagement perceived as incompatible with this attitude of ironic detachment.[60] The characteristic ambivalence praised by (largely white) critics is attacked by hooks as a negation of resistance and a refusal of commitment. hooks expresses unease over the ambivalence in the resistance to oppression.

At times he seems to be suggesting in the film that resistance to racism, sexism, and other forms of domination assumes the quality of spectacle and farce because the forces to be overcome are all-powerful, a rather despairing take. It is not surprising that some audiences miss the irony and think that the message is that one should focus on personal pleasure to have any satisfaction in life, since the oppression does not end.

The crux of hooks's argument is that Kureishi's politicized response is weakened because his 'irony is not always conveyed'. She contends that some audiences miss the irony and laugh, 'not in a critical or subversive way', but because they identified with Sammy's indifference to the dereliction of the race riots.[61] For hooks, the reactions of the white students at Yale she observed raise the issue of 'whether irony alone can be used to promote critical consciousness. It seems to pre-suppose a politically conscious viewer, one who can see both what is being shown and what is not.'[62] She asserts, 'Given the farcical elements in the film, one never knows quite when a scene should be viewed seriously'. hooks suggests that Kureishi's irony makes his politics ambivalent, particularly for people completely outside the political context. However, in assuming 'knowing' is always desirable, hooks projects a didactic intention on the writer that he self-consciously resists. She implicitly critiques Kureishi's negation of the didactic mode in his observation that 'Irony is the modern mode, a way of commenting on bleakness and cruelty without falling into dourness or didacticism'.[63] Elsewhere Kureishi insists it is futile to try to 'control an audience' and instead wants only 'to poke it up the nose as much as you can.'[64]

hooks's criticisms articulate the expectations of many readers (myself included) who seek, particularly in texts authored by minority artists a narrative of resistance that 'subverts or liberates' without ambiguity or contradiction.[65] The consistent feature in Kureishi's work is that he never gives you politics in the way you might anticipate but in an unexpected form. Just as Kureishi's *Laundrette* refuses to present positive images, *Sammy and Rosie* is no simple narrative of resistance. In a manner analogous to feminist projects, Kureishi opens up sites such as the sexual that are not always considered political. He is innovative in developing a political practice that cuts across

59

conventional formal categories. His films do not articulate alternatives, but subvert realist conventions to dramatize problems and conflicts, and put the onus on the viewer or reader to take a position. He is not concerned with consciously formulating propositions or political analysis and wants to raise debate rather than present didactic accounts. In contrast to the 'teaching' impulse implicit in hooks's framework, Kureishi dramatizes issues for the audience to think about, he does not want to do the work for them, which points to his use of a performative Brechtian aesthetic. Kureishi suggests 'films should be machines for generating interpretations...so we make them as ambiguous as possible; we want to make the audience think, hate, get angry'.[66] The provocative engagement his work engenders suggests he is successful in this.

3

Culture and Identity

'A funny kind of Englishman' (*BS* 3)

From the collaborative medium of film, with its particular constraints, Kureishi moves to the contrasting freedom of the novel to explore an unmediated relationship to the audience and a degree of interiority.[1] In contrast to his screenplays, Kureishi describes his first-person novel as 'much more internal ... an act of exposure'.[2] *The Buddha of Suburbia* (hereafter *Buddha*) is more autobiographical and lighter in tone than Kureishi's screenplays. The novel is a comic analysis of cultural moments of the seventies mediated through the narrator Karim Amir's expanding consciousness and coming of age as he leaves the suburbs for theatrical and sexual adventures in London and New York. In this way *Buddha* blends conventions of the picaresque novel and the *Bildungsroman*, with Karim's travels and encounters with an array of disparate characters driving his exploration of questions of identity. Kureishi's cutting satire finds its chief vehicle in the fictional narrative and in his quizzical first-person narrator, although it is tempered by an underlying tenderness. *Buddha* shows Kureishi's ability to integrate a comic, bawdy style with moments of seriousness and emotional depth. The punchy, idiomatic dialogue, variety of arresting characters and rapid pace give the novel its range, verve and creative energy.

Karim is the son of a white British mother Margaret and Indian father Haroon, and, as he puts it dryly, an 'Englishman born and bred almost' (*BS* 3). Karim straddles two cultures. On his father's side, there is Haroon's childhood friend Anwar, his wife Jeeta and their daughter Jamila, a committed feminist and anti-racist, Karim's best friend and sometime sexual partner, who is emotionally blackmailed into an arranged marriage to

Changez. On his mother's side there are his white suburban relations Jean and Ted 'two normal unhappy alcoholics' nicknamed Gin and Tonic (*BS* 33). The novel dramatizes the intersection of these colliding, absorbing social worlds. Although written from a raced perspective, describing racism in Britain from the point of view of a narrator of mixed parentage, the novel also explores masculinity, what it is like to be a British male growing up in the suburbs. Karim is a 'restless and easily bored' bisexual 17-year old whose ambitions and sexual desires are stifled in the suburbs (*BS* 3). Karim's bisexuality is implicitly presented as a parallel process to the slipping in and out of racialized categories. His first love is his hero at school, the beautiful, manipulative Charlie, who becomes a punk rock star. Charlie's vibrant, arty, ambitious mother Eva Kay fascinates Haroon (and Karim). Eva holds soirées for Haroon to show suburbanites 'The Path' to a more contemplative life, even if, as Karim observes 'Dad couldn't even find his way to Beckenham' (*BS* 13). Eva and Haroon's passionate affair leads to Haroon leaving Karim's mother. Karim moves in with his father and Eva and so makes his escape to London where life 'was bottomless in its temptations' (*BS* 8). He becomes an actor in 'alternative' theatre, but finds he is only offered 'ethnic' roles. The novel recounts Karim's escapades, his disappointment in love and evasion of politics. This energetic narrative's vitality flags towards the end. In keeping with Kureishi's resistance to clear-cut conclusions *Buddha* closes ambiguously with Karim both 'happy and miserable', hoping to learn to 'live more deeply' in the future, as he sits 'in the centre of this old city that [he] loved' (*BS* 284). The novel's concerns over identity are not resolved in the manner usually characteristic of the *Bildungsroman*.[3] Kureishi's irony imbues the narrative with alternative meanings and gives expression to the novel's polyphony. Its multiple narratives are filtered through Karim's consciousness, but the preponderance of direct speech creates an impression of intimacy and immediacy. Farcical episodes disrupt but never completely subvert the novel's realism. The text's multiple perspectives are reinforced by its linguistic pluralism, freewheeling between a range of registers.

The novel continues Kureishi's explorations of identity within a multicultural, multiracial Britain fraught with racial tensions. Kureishi subverts notions of identity and culture as immutable, authentic and fixed in conceptions of origins. While the text emphasizes that identities are, to an extent, culturally and politically constructed by stressing the role of performance, it is sceptical of questions of identity being 'resolved' in performance and maps its limitations. In contrast to the earlier screenplays, set in the eighties, Karim's picaresque adventures span the seventies. The novel marks the transition from the tail end of sixties hippie culture, the Beatles' interest in India, flares and the Stones, to the Sex Pistols and the punk scene. It ends with the 1979 election, the Labour party's fall and the beginning of Thatcher's era. *Buddha* foregrounds Kureishi's special talent for evoking a period in terms of fashion, music and transitional youth culture.[4] In the pub, we see 'ageing Teddy boys in drape coats, with solid sculpted quiffs like ships' prows. There were a few vicious Rockers too, in studded leather and chains bands.... And there were a couple of skinheads with their girls, in brogues, Levi's, Crombies and braces' (*BS* 75).

Kureishi's vivid recreation of seventies England is no nostalgic revival: he juxtaposes the escalation of vicious racist attacks (and the emerging popular anti-fascist politics that rose to combat it) with the middle-class taste for India and exoticism. The novel's backdrop is an era of unemployment, class antagonism 'strikes, marches, wage-claims' (*BS* 259). Although the novel is set in the seventies, in the dramatization of its protagonists' differing political orientations the text anticipates the breakdown of Left politics and the waning of the anti-fascist coalitions that occurred in the eighties. Karim's resistance to any form of collective politics prefigures the movement away from the broad-based anti-racism that Jamila embraces, and the decline of Left party-politics that fellow actor Terry espouses as a member of the Socialist Workers Party. Karim's trajectory maps the trend of the future which readers reading the narrative in the nineties would identity with. The novel embodies an underlying tension between the cultural and political spheres that Karim and Jamila respectively inhabit and represent. Does *Buddha*'s emphasis on cultural representation move the focus away from collective politics and displace political action in favour of the cultural domain? To what extent is the text self-critical of this? Or does it stage alternatives that are interrelated?

The novel will be examined from these perspectives.

Kureishi's novel depicts all characters, white, black, racist and anti-racist, with dry, satiric humour and in uncompromisingly farcical terms, including the selfish, self-deprecating, self-conscious narrator Karim. In this way *Buddha* illustrates two defining features of Kureishi's work. First, it exemplifies the liminality of Kureishi's position as an 'in-between' or insider/ outsider, which relates to the ironic distance that characterizes the novel, and is linked to Kureishi's specular function. From this position as an 'in-between', Kureishi (via his deeply autobiographical Karim) holds up a self-ironizing and satirical mirror to the white and minority communities that he moves between. At the same time, Kureishi can ironize both communities because he is positioned as an insider of both. However, although his ironic distance gives an impression of detachment, Kureishi mocks what he feels strongly about. While he ironizes all political positions, this should not be read as a summary dismissal. This pervasive ironizing is linked to the second characteristic: the subversive, anarchic streak in Karim/Kureishi that resists all forms of authority. Karim/Kureishi is not simply positioned against the dominant culture, he takes that form of resistance as a given: he questions all forms of subcultures, affiliations, and collectivities.

In the novel, Kureishi satirizes the milieus of his youth, lampooning white suburbia's parochialism and crude racism: 'We're with Enoch' (*BS* 40). Kureishi's astute caricatures of the 'radical' theatre directors Shadwell and Pyke and their appropriation of racial issues and manipulation of Karim expose more insidious forms of racism. Through Pyke, Kureishi parodies the intellectual Left's subordination of race under class 'the only subject there is in England' (*BS* 164). Kureshi mocks the white liberal embracing of India that bears the racist taints of orientalism, such as Eva's attempt to identify Haroon as an embodiment of eastern spirituality and the way her attraction to him is predicated on his conforming to the role of 'exotic' other. A similar taste for exoticism lurks in Karim's girlfriend Helen's desire to comfort Haroon: 'But this is your home' ... 'We like you being here. You benefit our country with your traditions' (*BS* 74). Eager, well-meaning liberals are not spared Kureishi's self-betraying dialogue and eye for revealing detail.

Kureishi mercilessly targets the suburban obsession with houses and displays of wealth, where 'it was said that when people drowned they saw not their lives but their double glazing flashing before them' (BS 23). Ted and Jean, who live in the more affluent part of Chislehurst, are depicted as a suburban couple who 'measured people only in terms of power and money' (BS 34). Kureishi is equally critical of the insularity of Anwar and his wife Jeeta, who are solely preoccupied with their grocery store and 'knew nothing of the outside world' and for whom the 'idea of enjoyment had passed . . . by'. Their way of life is positioned as the other extreme of the white suburbanites' materialism: 'I don't know how much money they had. But if they had anything they must have buried it, because they never bought any of the things people in Chislehurst would exchange their legs for: velvet curtains, stereos, Martinis, electric lawnmowers, double glazing' (BS 51).

Kureishi laughs at the flaws and contradictions of all his characters, a political move in his continued assertion that minorities are not a separate category, to be protected from satire. Kureishi mocks what he sees as pious, humourless forms of anti-racism, which suggest otherwise. So the migrant's nostalgia for 'home' is ridiculed. As they grow old, Haroon and Anwar return to an imaginary India inwardly without wishing to visit it (BS 64). Jamila's husband Changez and the Japanese sex-worker Shinko missed their respective homelands desperately, 'but not enough to get on a plane and go there' (BS 210). Kureishi's comic treatment of minorities once more treads a precariously fine line between humour and caricature, illustrated in the portrayal of the 'slightly dim' Changez, the unwanted husband Jamila's father imports from Bombay who at first appears as a figure of pure ridicule, a Peter Sellers stereotype. His Indian English and sexual aspirations are parodied. Jamila reluctantly agrees to marry him, but does not let him touch her. As the story progresses Changez's complexity and substance is developed. He remains a rich comic presence and generates much of the novel's wild humour: Anwar's death is the result of the farcical set piece where Changez defends himself from his father-in-law's fury and inadvertently knocks him unconscious with a large pink dildo. However, Changez moves from being a caricature to become one of the novel's strongest characters. He surprises everyone when, after moving into a commune with Jamila, he becomes the devoted carer of the baby Jamila has with another man. Fat, balding, with a deformed arm, Changez's plea when Jamila refuses to kiss him that the 'rights' of 'ugly bastards' are being ignored in this right-on 'house of holy socialists' is both touching and funny (*BS* 277–8).

Similarly, Kureishi subverts the potential cliché of the novel's main sub plot, where Anwar becomes a 'principle of absolute patriarchal authority' and goes on a hunger strike to force Jamila into this arranged marriage (*BS* 64). As Nahem Yousaf observes, the family appears to conform to 'the "popular" image of the Asian family [involving] tropes of the authoritarian patriarch, the unhappy arranged marriage and the Asian woman as submissive victim...[already] clearly inscribed within the minds of the reading public'.[5] The portrayal of the militant feminist Jamila with her 'temper and Angela Davis's beliefs' is far from that of a stereotyped submissive victim (*BS* 57). However, Kureishi uses Anwar's actions to thematize the politics of the representation of black minorities within the novel. When Karim wants to base his character on Anwar's recent behaviour in an improvised play with his drama group, Tracey, a young British African-Caribbean actress, objects because, she argues, it depicts 'black and Asian people' as 'irrational, ridiculous' and 'hysterical' (*BS* 180). Kureishi shows the representation of minorities as a site of contested negotiations within the minority communities themselves, rather than between the dominant majority and minority communities: the white members of the 'group listened but kept out of the discussion. This thing was suddenly between "minorities"' (*BS* 180).[6] Tracey says:

> '...Your picture is what white people already think of us. That we're funny, with strange habits and weird customs. To the white man we're already a people without humanity, and then you go and have Anwar madly waving his stick at white boys....You show us as unorganized aggressors...'
> 'But this sounds like censorship.'
> 'We have to protect our culture at this time, Karim. Don't you agree?'
> 'No. Truth has a higher value.'
> 'Pah. Truth. Who defines it? What truth? It's a white truth you're defending here. It's white truth we're discussing. (*BS* 180–81)

This is one way in which Kureishi's novel retains the dialogic quality of his previous screenplays, with characters articulating different positions opposing the narrative voice. Once more, Kureishi's text performs a conflict, pushing the onus on the reader to decide and take a position. At the same time, Kureishi presents the debate between Karim and Tracey in terms of the autonomy of art versus censorship, a loaded term associated with authoritarianism. Karim's defence of his portrayal has many resonances with Kureishi's own views expressed elsewhere. Kureishi has described Spike Lee as performing a form of self-censorship, which is why he will not show black Americans 'doing drugs in his films'. In contrast, Kureishi insists that 'I won't be tied. I can't.... Otherwise, it is bollocks. It's censorship. It's just censorship.'[7] Thus, both within and outside the text, the position of the quintessential liberal artist in society, who remains unaccountable to these understandable reactions, is asserted. Kureishi refuses any notion of the artist as 'responsible'.[8]

Karim implies that Tracey's subordinate position in the network of class and racial hierarchies affects the way the rest of the drama group respond to her: 'As she continued, I looked around the group...I could see the others were prepared to agree with Tracey. It was difficult to disagree with someone whose mother you'd found kneeling in front of a middle-class house with a bucket and mop' (BS 180–81). In contrast to Karim, Tracey has the 'authority' of the black working class, although it is Pyke's authority as director that forces Karim to rethink his character. However, although Tracey assails Karim's stereotypical portrayals (echoed, as we will see, by Jamila), her objections appear to be raised to provide and acknowledge an alternative perspective only to be then rejected by Karim. He goes on to create an equally caricatured figure, Tariq, based on Changez: 'a wretched comic character' through whom Karim portrays 'the sexual ambition and humiliation of an Indian in England' (BS 220). As Spivak implies, Tracey's political maturity is contrasted with Karim's political naïveté, nevertheless Tracey is also satirized as humourless and her reference to 'white truth' and the need to 'protect our culture at this time' is presented as a proto-separatist position (BS 181).[9] This separatism is echoed in Jamila's reply to Karim's request to discuss her crisis in front of one of his white girlfriends: 'Yes, if you want to expose our culture as being ridiculous and our people as old-fashioned, extreme and narrow-minded' (*BS* 71). While their comments are deployed to ironize Kureishi/Karim's stance, their objections are in turn ironized as stemming from defensive conceptions of culture as the property of discrete 'racial' subjects.[10] In this way, the politics of representation is examined in terms of disputes over culture.

CULTURE AND ETHNIC ABSOLUTISM

Explorations of culture form a central subject of the novel. *Buddha* subverts hermetically sealed notions of culture and 'ethnic absolutism' manifested in conceptions of the irreducible, immutable cultural differences between white and black people that Paul Gilroy suggests anti-racists, multiculturalists and new racists alike revert to.[11] *Buddha* contests reified conceptions of culture as a given essence inherited, handed down from generation to generation. Instead, Kureishi continues his examination of the many different ways in which young Asians in Britain reconstitute what is called 'tradition'. Some have attempted to 'slough off their origins', like Karim's brother Amar who 'called himself Allie to avoid racial trouble' (*BS* 19).[12] Rather than perpetuating or pursuing a discrete ethnic identity, Karim is immersed in youth subculture that is itself a way of avoiding racialized environments. Jamila draws from a range of feminist intellectuals – Simone de Beauvoir, Germaine Greer and Kate Millett – to educate herself and develop a critical consciousness. Jamila's political orientation and aspirations are particularly inspired by the defiant political and cultural expression of the black power movements in America, especially the writings of Angela Davis as well as Malcolm X and Baldwin. This dovetails with Gilroy's argument that black British 'culture does not develop along ethnically absolute lines but in complex, dynamic patterns of syncretism in which new definitions of what it means to be black emerge from raw materials provided by black populations elsewhere in the diaspora'.[13] Kureishi explores a range of positions between polarities of assimilation and being consumed by tradition. His characters articulate difference, but not from the margins or enclaves: Jamila with her radical commune is immersed in all aspects of life and political struggles in contemporary Britain.

Any attempts to be culturally 'authentic' are exposed as farce. Take for example the new-found, spurious spirituality of Haroon, 'a renegade Muslim masquerading as a Buddhist' (*BS* 16). The novel pokes fun at the way Haroon discovers and cultivates his Otherness (from 'books on Buddhism, Sufism, Confucianism and Zen which he had bought at the Oriental bookshop... off Charing Cross Road') and stages it to suit white audiences, *after* coming to Britain (*BS* 5). Haroon's vague, pretentious dispensation of 'Eastern philosophy' is sent up, as is the white suburban credulity that an 'authentic' spiritual India exists and that it finds innate expression in Haroon. Anwar's impatience with Haroon's esoteric philosophizing about 'the China-things', and admonition to 'Wake up! What about getting some promotion so that Margaret can wear some nice clothes', underscores the falsity of an easy binarism of an East/spiritual and West/materialistic dichotomy (*BS* 27). *Buddha* implicitly redefines culture not as an originary essence, but as a resource that for example Anwar invokes in an attempt to assert patriarchal authority. Anwar's metamorphosis is presented as a performance: Anwar suddenly starts 'behaving like a Muslim' (*BS* 64). Essentialist notions of cultural identity are repudiated by the emphasis on the performance of the ethnic dimension of identity. This appears to anticipate Judith Butler's work on gender 'masquerade', which some critics have extended to similarly contest a supposed coherence between biologically inscribed categories and ethnicity. However, Butler's performative gender is not synonymous with 'performance' or 'theatre', both of which would assume an actor who initiates its gendered acts.[14] Butler's concept contrasts with Kureishi's representations of the conscious performance of ethnicity, wherein a notion of a residual sense of self behind the performance, however elusive, remains.

IDENTITY AS PERFORMANCE

Haroon's assertion of cultural difference that follows his initial attempt at assimilation is presented as a performance. Having 'spent years trying to be more of an Englishman, to be less risibly conspicuous... now he was putting it back in spade-loads': 'hissing his s's and exaggerating his Indian accent' in order to become the buddha of suburbia (*BS* 21). Analogously, Karim tries to reinvent himself in class terms when he moves from the suburbs to London. When his white, upper-class Bohemian girlfriend Eleanor describes his South London 'street-voice' and 'accent' as 'cute... different to my voice of course', Karim resolves to lose his accent: 'whatever it was, it would go. I would speak like her. It wasn't difficult. I'd left my world; I had to, to get on' (*BS* 178). This is paralleled by Eva's more aggressive attempts 'to scour that suburban stigmata right off her body' (*BS* 134). Kureishi underlines the way Karim tries on a series of personas by making him an actor, which is 'a profession of mutation'.[15] Karim's theatrical performances of Anwar and Changez/Tariq and the invention of their characters exaggerate the processes of construction of a sense of self.

Karim's ethnic identity is also partly constructed for him. The theatrical roles Karim is asked to play (first Kipling's Mowgli and then an immigrant) mirror the way society attempts to define racialized minorities in terms of reductive identities. Kureishi is showing how difficult it is 'for a person of colour to evade the definitions settled upon him'.[16] He satirizes the insidious cultural racism of theatre director Shadwell who wants to impose on Karim a 'destiny' 'which is to be a half-caste in England. That must be complicated for you to accept – belonging nowhere, wanted nowhere' (*BS* 141). Shadwell's objectification of Karim is underlined when he coerces Karim to appear more 'Indian', to put on an 'authentic' Indian accent and wear 'shit-brown' make-up over his 'creamy' skin (*BS* 146). When Karim objects to having to adopt an Indian accent, Shadwell insists: 'Karim, you have been cast for authenticity and not for experience' (*BS* 147). On the whole, Karim succumbs to the objectification, occasionally disrupting it when he 'sends up' the Indian accent and persona imposed on him by 'relapsing into Cockney at odd times' (*BS* 158). Karim's entrée into the theatrical world is based on problematic notions of ethnicity, race and culture. Kureishi points to the way that black actors and actresses in the seventies were considered 'chic' and were required to act out essentialized stereotypes or (as Jamila points out) pander 'to prejudices...and clichés about Indians' (*BS* 157).[17] As I have suggested, Karim continues to cooperate with forms of cultural racism when he lands a part in Pyke's 'avant-garde' theatre production and creates his own character, a more contemporary but equally stereotyped figure of the post-colonial immigrant. Significantly the audiences warm to Karim's caricature of Changez/Tariq, finding it 'hilarious and honest' (*BS* 228). In a characteristically opportunistic and pragmatic manner, Karim defends his role: 'I'm an actor. It's a job' (*BS* 232).

Kureishi differentiates between the nature of Haroon's and Karim's self-conceptions and stagings of identity. Kureishi explores the impact on identity formation of the different formative experiences of first-generation immigrants and their British-born children. The first generation have grown up in a society where their right to be there was not questioned.[18] In contrast to Jamila and Karim, Haroon's identity is taken for granted, 'it just existed' (*BS* 213). While Haroon may have 'lived in the West for most of [his] life... [he remains] to all intents and purposes an Indian man. [He] will never be anything but an Indian' (*BS* 263). So, in Kureishi's representation of Haroon's performance there remains, however imaginary and indefinable, a notion of a residual sense of self. In contrast, Karim reveals a more fraught, unstable subjectivity. His fractured, divided and contradictory sense of self stems from the opposition between societal conceptions of his identity and his self-perception. In their formative years, Karim and Jamila experiment with a range of identities because they are not allowed to be English: 'sometimes we were French, Jammie and I, and other times we went black American. The thing was, we were supposed to be English, but to the English we were always wogs and nigs and Pakis and the rest of it' (*BS* 53). Here Kureishi's irony subverts dominant constructions by implying other meanings. Karim's awakening sense of identification with the Indian community to which he partly belongs, that he has hitherto repressed, is presented as an important epiphany that occurs during Anwar's funeral:

But I did feel, looking at these strange creatures now – the Indians – that in some way these were my people, and that I'd spent my life denying or avoiding that fact. I felt ashamed and incomplete at the same time, as if half of me were missing, as if I'd been colluding with my enemies, those whites who wanted Indians to be like them. Partly I blamed Dad for this. After all...for most of his life, he'd never shown any interest in going back to India. He was always honest about this: he preferred England in every way. ...He wasn't proud of his past, but he wasn't unproud of it either; it just existed, and there wasn't any point in fetishizing it, as some liberals and Asian radicals liked to do. So if I wanted the additional personality bonus of an Indian past, I would have to create it. (*BS* 212–13)

However, while he identifies (and the emphasis is on a physical identification) with 'these people', he is culturally distinct from them, as the last sentence makes clear. There is no sense that his dilemma over his cultural identity is over or that he can revert to his 'roots'. This passage suggests that in terms of the essentialism versus culturalism debates, Kureishi's position eludes both polarities. Ultimately unlike Haroon, Karim is represented as a spectral figure with a void at the centre, desiring a sense of self that he lacks. With Karim we see *identity as performance*. Karim suggests that the process of creating the character of Changez/Tariq made him *feel* 'more solid myself, and not as if my mind was just a kind of cinema for myriad impressions and emotions to flicker through' (*BS* 217). As Spivak observes, 'We are not surprised that Karim is represented as creatively happy when he puts together his stage Indian. The intimate enemy, a violation that enables'.[19]

This raises the question, to what extent is performance empowering? Does it help to solve Karim's implicit identity crisis? This search for a coherent sense of self forms the thematic link between *Buddha* and Kipling's *Kim* (1901), wherein the question 'who is Kim?' is insistently and more explicitly articulated but never settled. 'Karim' verbally echoes 'Kim' and both protagonists are neither Indian nor English but insiders/outsiders who perform identity. Many commentators suggest that Haroon and Karim's role-playing leads them to greater self-knowledge.[20] But while Karim feels the invention 'added up the elements of my life' (*BS* 217), Kureishi implies when the performance (theatrical or otherwise) ends the

72

question of subjectivity remains uncertain. The need to create a self from 'the odd mixture of continents and blood, of here and there, of belonging and not' persists (*BS* 3). *Buddha* ends with Karim 'happy and miserable' and confused as ever over his cultural dilemma (*BS* 284). For Karim (as for Kim) the question 'who am I?' remains unanswered. For Kureishi, far from resolving identity performance reveals it as bogus, ridiculous and meaningless. Kureishi sends up the postmodern culture of identity as commodity. Charlie Hero invents a working-class cockney accent in America and is shown 'selling Englishness, and getting a lot of money for it' (*BS* 247). Although set in the seventies just before the economic boom of the eighties, Karim, Charlie and Haroon's commodification of the performance of cultural identity mocks the profile of the Thatcherite market-oriented eighties of consumer activity as well as the credulity of the consumers. While Haroon and Karim respectively dismiss 'the materialistic age' and the 'carnival of consumerism' that was beginning to dawn, they are clearly part of it (*BS* 65).

The text outlines the limited nature of the 'subversive' potential of performance. On the one hand, the simulation of cultural identity suggests a degree of agency on the part of the performer: he/she in control of his/her self-construction rather than being defined. However, Haroon's act simultaneously serves to reinforce dominant expectations that such an origin exists and ironically contributes to a form of ethnic absolutism. Haroon substitutes his initial attempt at assimilation for an assertion of cultural difference. Yet, in responding to the vogue for the spiritual sustenance of the exotic East, this 'abrogation' or assertion of difference is dictated to according to the norms of the host society and remains a form of assimilation. This assimilation through a form of abrogation problematizes the polarization of these terms and suggests that the assimilation/abrogation paradigm can be better described as a dialectical relation.[21]

BEYOND PERFORMANCE AND CONSTRUCTIONS OF IDENTITY

Paul Gilroy has drawn attention to the potential dangers within the counter-arguments to racial essentialism. Gilroy suggests that 'in leaving racial essentialism behind by viewing "race" itself as a social and cultural construction', this emphasis 'has been insufficiently alive to the lingering power of specifically racialised forms of power and subordination'.[22] In his fore-grounding of the construction of ethnic identities, does Kureishi participate in this erasure? While Karim perceives the Indian aspect of his identity as an 'additional personality bonus' he can create or augment at will, Kureishi shows it cannot be as easily dismissed (BS 213). Neither Haroon nor Karim can escape being perceived as black. Kureishi shows how their identities are defined by colour, a privileged visible signifier of difference. So Haroon tries to avoid getting 'stones and ice-pops full of piss lobbed at him by schoolboys' and Karim suffered racial bullying at school and is labelled as 'a little coon', one of the 'niggers' and 'blackies'. Helen's father tells him she doesn't go out with 'wogs' (BS 28, 40).[23] Buddha's most urgent passages draw attention to 'racialised forms of power and subordination'. In the compelling delineation of the growth of the National Front and 'Paki-bashing', the novel depicts the oppression of racial hatred and its impact on Jamila's family:

> The area in which Jamila lived was closer to London than our suburbs, and far poorer. It was full of neo-fascist groups, thugs who had their own pubs, clubs and shops. On Saturdays they'd be out in the High Street selling their newspapers and pamphlets.... At night they roamed the streets, beating Asians and shoving shit and burning rags through their letterboxes. Frequently the mean, white, hating faces had public meetings and the Union Jacks were paraded through the streets, protected by police. There was no evidence that these people would go away – no evidence that their power would diminish rather than increase. The lives of Anwar, Jeeta and Jamila were pervaded by the fear of violence. ...Jeeta kept buckets of water around her bed in case the shop was firebombed in the night. (BS 56)

Significantly, this level of racism is less immediate for Karim, who is distanced from it in class terms.

Buddha explores competing ways of combating racism through its dramatization of Jamila's arguments with Karim. Not only does Jamila condemn Karim's participation in racist productions, she dismisses Karim's preoccupation with cultural representation rather than political action. Jamila mocks ' these actresses and such-like vain fools. The world burns...they try and put the burning world on the stage. It never occurs to them to dowse the flames' (BS 176).[24] She reminds Karim, as he gets seduced into his theatrical world of the 'rich and powerful', about 'the world of ordinary people and the shit they have to deal with – unemployment, bad housing, boredom' (BS 195). She is committed to fight the cause of 'oppressed people, like our people in this racist country, who face violence every day' (BS 108). So, Karim is defined in contrast to the politically committed anti-racist Jamila, who in many ways appears to act as the novel's moral centre and provides a critique of Karim's wavering commitment to the anti-fascist movement. (In contrast to Karim, her sustained commitment is presented as contributing to a more stable sense of self.) While Karim is 'angered' by the racial attack on Changez – and admires the activists and respects Jamila's 'feminism...the sense of self and the fight it engendered...as she went forward, an Indian woman, to live a useful life in white England' (BS 216) – he chooses not to embrace activism. He fails to turn up to the march protesting against the National Front rally because of his pursuit of Eleanor. Once again, Kureishi dramatizes the shifting nature of preoccupations or priorities, and how desire makes political commitment ambivalent. Jamila draws attention to her white boyfriend, who received injuries from 'a bottle in the face' at the demonstration, to underline Karim's contrasting evasion (BS 232).

Although within the novel Karim's failures and immersion in theatre are critiqued, the text works at two levels. We need to look beyond the dramatized positions of Jamila and Karim to see what the text is doing. The *effect* of *Buddha* is to show how racism operates within culture and infiltrates the formation of knowledge. It positions the cultural domain as integral to the political, not separate or antithetical as Jamila implies. In showing this, the novel implies that, like feminism, anti-racism needs to be deployed at different levels, even though within the text Karim neglects both. Ultimately perhaps Karim and Jamila do not occupy mutually exclusive positions but are staging alternatives that are interrelated. In juxtaposing their positions, the text mutually modifies both.

Furthermore, characteristically, the critique of Karim is not so clear-cut. It appears intermittently in keeping with a liberal tradition of presenting alternative points of view. It is London's acting circles, the lure of drugs, sex and excitement that engage Karim and occupy the centre of the novel: Karim's pursuit of detached liberal individualism is privileged structurally and perhaps thematically. The self-deprecating Karim generates humour and sympathy, drawing us in to 'naturalize', if not endorse, his selfishness: 'compared to Jammie I was, as a militant, a real shaker and a trembler' (BS 53). We are meant to admire Jamila, but we are subtly encouraged to identify with Karim, an identification encouraged by the first-person voice. It is almost as if Kureishi's comparison presents Jamila as how people should be, and Karim as how they are.

Critical responses emphasize Karim 'actively trying to resist the clutches of a paternalistic and tyrannical racist discourse'.[25] What is overlooked is Karim's scepticism, suspicion and ambivalence to all forms of affiliation, collectivities, organizations and authority. This anarchic strain in Karim/Kureishi's political irreverence is most evident in this novel, reminiscent of Joe Orton's anarchic black humour. Characteristically, Kureishi is not concerned to provide political solutions, and instead highlights the blindspots in a range of positions on the political spectrum. This includes those espoused by Tracey and Jamila. Where 'radical' whites can critique aspects of whiteness, Tracey immediately reads Karim's portrayals as evidence of the extent to which he 'hates [himself] and all black people' (BS 180). The novel is marked with witty subversions of Jamila's feminist politics. Changez's sex sessions, experimenting positions described in Harold Robbins's fiction with the Japanese sex-worker Shinko, appear doomed when Jamila forms a friendship with Shinko and accuses Changez of patriarchal exploitation. Jamila suggests that Shinko should become a gardener instead. However, as Changez later reports to Karim: 'But thank Christ Almighty in heaven, they realised Shinko was exploiting me. I was the victim and all, so it was soon back to business as usual' (BS 183). Similarly Karim's fellow actor Terry's brand of socialism is satirized. Karim is let down by Terry's failure to stand up to the authoritarian director Shadwell. Terry is mocked for preferring instead to spout class-based rhetoric. Terry's ideology is made an easy target, presented as a rather stereotypical version of Marxism. Karim objects to the 'rigid...way of seeing', 'the flood of opinion, the certainty, the easy talk about Cuba and Russia and the economy, because beneath the hard structure of words was an abyss of ignorance and not-knowing; and in a sense, of not wanting to know' (BS 241). With a typical ironic twist, Terry ends up playing a policeman in a television series. While Karim resists all forms of authority, he also resists strong bonds and commitment. It seems that Kureishi's male protagonists are always avoiding and resisting commitment of any kind. Perhaps Kureishi is not exclusively interested in overtly politicized positions, but is also concerned to explore loyalty (and disloyalty in Karim's relationship with Changez) and commitment in a spectrum of relationships. Karim's lack of political solidarity with anti-racism is just one of the bonds about which he is ambivalent; his relationship with his family is another example. The ambivalence of belonging and the exploration of Haroon Amir's making and breaking of relationships anticipate *Intimacy*.

APPENDIX: *LONDON KILLS ME* 1991

As we have seen, Kureishi contests the 'burden of representation' in *Laundrette* and *Sammy and Rosie*, and incorporates it as theme in *Buddha*. In his subsequent screenplay, *London Kills Me* (which he directed for the first time), he further displaces an aspect of the burden of representation: specifically, the requirement to explore questions of race and depict minority experiences. Although *London Kills Me* has a multiracial cast, it focuses on white homeless youth. In an interview at the time of its release, Kureishi explains: 'It seems to me progress to *assume* that we live in a mixed society. Before it was your job to say: "Oh, by the way, there are amazing people here who do live here and are part of Britain". Now we can integrate that into our work while not forgetting it.'[26] While Kureishi says there is no point talking about race now, in another interview he admits that after *Buddha* he had exhausted race as a subject for 'the time being'.[27] He has always justifiably asserted his right to explore other subjects and resists being confined to what is demarcated as the ethnic minority artist's terrain.

77

London Kills Me revolves around Clint (Justin Chadwick), a member of a drug-dealing posse, and his quest to find some acceptable footwear for a job as a waiter in a trendy diner that will enable him to go straight. The film delineates the triangular relationship between Clint, white Irish Sylvie (Emer McCourt) who has tried rehabilitation, and Muffdiver (Steven Mackintosh) the posse's leader, an ambitious, violent hustler who wants to expand the business. The one member of the posse of Asian origin, Bike (named so because he is inseparable from his mountain bike), is a strangely silent figure. The group break into a flat in London's Whitehall Gardens and squat. When Clint steals some money from Muffdiver, an advance from their main supplier Mr G., a fight breaks out. The next day Clint takes Sylvie on an outing to the country; uninvited, the rest of the posse joins them. This visit to Clint's estranged mother's home fleshes out the hints we have been given about Clint's traumatic childhood. On their return, Mr G. decides to evict and punish the squatters. Muffdiver and Sylvie flee London disguised as goths (wearing deathly white make-up and dressed from head to toe in black). Clint steals a pair of cowboy boots, only to find they belong to his prospective employer, but finally gets the job anyway. The ending is characteristically ambiguous: it marks the end of his hard, haphazard life on the streets. At the same time, there is a suggestion of a loss of vitality in his conformity, in the obsequious way Clint attends the diners.

In this raw portrayal of this group of young homeless addicts on the streets of Notting Hill, Kureishi continues his exploration of disaffected youth, homelessness, street subculture, and his unveiling of London's underside. The fractious hostilities between members of the posse contrast with the surreal, idyllic portrayal of the commune in *Sammy and Rosie*. The film also underscores Kureishi's fascination with London's diverse, chaotic mix of Sufi centres (run by the charming Dr Bubba), gays, blacks, whites, and tourists. As Sandhu observes, Kureishi's techniques of 'juxtaposition and collage are the ideal aesthetic modes for incarnating this higgledy-piggledy commotion of a metropolis'.[28] In contrast to *Sammy and Rosie*, Kureishi wanted to make *London Kills Me* a simpler, less ideologically oriented and less crowded film, and move away from politics embedded in and articulated by the characters as in *Laundrette*.[29]

78

The result is a film that for many reviewers embodies the aimlessness of its characters and lacks a coherent tone. One reviewer observes that the artificial pattern in the search for shoes sits uneasily with the convincing dialogue and realistic West London setting.[30] At the same time, the technique of generic bricolage, mixing documentary naturalism with fairy-tale motifs subverts realist conventions, and reflects the fragmented outlook of the characters.

Although less rooted in its political context than his earlier films, *London Kills Me* recreates the energetic drug scene and the extremes of the late eighties: the yuppies who come to the diner are juxtaposed with the economically disenfranchised on the streets. The affluence of the token champagne radical Headley (who exploits Clint for drugs and sexual favours) is contrasted with the scarcity of the group's existence. However, the posse is not victimized and the film hints at the resilience, 'strength and determination you need when you've got nothing'. When Clint's stepfather accuses the group of being 'slaves of sensation', he is told that his way of life is as much 'slavery, habit, repetition' (*LKM* 59). The film does not moralize or glamorize drug-taking: there is a particularly painful, memorable scene where Sylvie injects herself in the groin.

Like *Buddha*, the film foregrounds music, clothes and style. It shows the characters experimenting with disguises and dramatizes London's potential for self-reinvention. Philip Dodd suggestively describes *London Kills Me* as a 'historical film about several generations, told through style'. He refers to 'Clint's macho Teddy boy stepfather with his Elvis obsession...there's the Bohemian 60's group with their cowboy boots, wine bars and music; and there's the young with their raves'. Kureishi suggests this implicit approach stems from the way he measures out his 'own life in pop music'. He describes it as 'a way of looking at history that young people would immediately understand. They have a fantastic knowledge of the history of pop music and see the world through that'.[31] We see a similar impulse behind the structuring of Kureishi's subsequent project, *The Faber Book of Pop* (1995). Here Kureishi and Savage present 'the alternative history of our time told from the standpoint of popular music, which is as good a position as any to look from, since pop, intersecting with issues of class, race and particularly gender, has been at the centre of post-war culture' (*F*, p. xix).

Kureishi's directorial debut was a critical and commercial failure. It was unfavourably compared to his earlier collaborations with Frears. Kaleta suggests an 'ominous undertow' lurked in some of the negative reviews of *London Kills Me* – 'namely, an apparent disapproval of the fact that Kureishi dared to tell the story of a *white* street-boy's experiences'.[32] While critics do tend to pigeonhole Kureishi as a minority artist, criticisms of *London Kills Me* focused on Kureishi's lack of control over his material as a *director*. *The Times* is representative in its suggestion that 'Kureishi's anger and insights do not always find a clear focus'. The film lacked 'a strong director to weave a clear path through London's raffish street life and swing dynamically between jostling moods. Kureishi displays little cinematic sense, with character and incident flung at the screen as if the words are not enough'.[33] Kureishi's initial shift from race was combined with his first attempt to direct.[34] As we will see, this move from race was achieved with greater success in his novella and short stories in the late nineties.

4

Muslimophobia

I didn't want to write a book that took sides. I'm interested in all sides of the argument. (Kureishi, 1995)[1]

This chapter examines Kureishi's representations of British Asian Muslims in the context of the racialization of British Muslim identities in the aftermath of the Rushdie affair (1989) and the Gulf War (1991). Tariq Modood's delineation of contemporary cultural racism against Muslims in Britain provides useful insights into the contexts in which Kureishi's novel *The Black Album* (hereafter *Black Album*) and screenplay *My Son the Fanatic* (hereafter *My Son*) are both produced and received. Modood defines cultural racism as the forms of prejudice that exclude and racialize culturally different ethnic minorities. As Modood suggests, Britain's shifting racialized boundaries are beginning to include certain culturally assimilated South Asian and African-Caribbean (middle-class) values, but continue to exclude and racialize culturally 'different' Asians, Arabs, and non-white Muslims.[2] Modood demonstrates that Britain's South Asian Muslims, particularly its Pakistani and Bangladeshi communities, are the most alienated, 'socially deprived and racially harassed group'.[3] Modood examines why Muslims are portrayed as a 'radical assault upon British values, a threat to the state and an enemy to good race relations'.[4] He suggests cultural racism is particularly aggressive towards minorities 'sufficiently numerous to reproduce [themselves] as a community'. It is hostile to communities with a distinctive and cohesive value system, which can be perceived as an alternative, and possible challenge, to the 'norm' and to those who wish to maintain and assert their cultural distinctiveness in public (for example, visible markers such as wearing the veil).[5] British Asian Muslims are perceived as the minority most resistant to assimilation. British Muslims' mass protests against Rushdie's *The Satanic Verses* provided a focal point for anti-Muslim racism. A recent Commission for Racial Equality survey, revealed that the younger Muslims in the group were acutely aware of the stereotypes of Islam that prevail in British society, and were at pains to emphasize the positive aspects of their religion and culture.[6] Modood makes the important point that discourses that see Muslims as a problem or a threat are not confined to an extreme fringe, popular prejudice or the right wing. As we will see, they can be implicit or explicit in both élite and progressive discourses.[7]

While Kureishi's *My Beautiful Laundrette* articulates a range of heterogeneous positions and diversifies representations of ethnic minorities, to differing degrees both *Black Album* and *My Son*'s stereotypical portraits of British Asian Muslims are circumscribed within narrow polarities. Kureishi's creative portrayals of British Muslims illustrate the extent to which he falls into 'the trap of specularity'. As we have seen, his work does not present an undiscriminating picture of the dominant majority. However, he uncritically reflects and embodies rather than questions its predominant fears, prejudices and perceptions of devout British Muslims as 'fundamentalists', constructed as particularly threatening in the West. His caricatures further objectify this already objectified group, whilst reinscribing dominant liberalism as the norm. Unlike *Laundrette*, where conceptions of both white and minority communities are challenged and unsettled, this recent work often simply reaffirms the values of the dominant group. *Black Album* and *My Son* illustrate the degree to which Kureishi's work is implicitly directed at the dominant majority and constructed in terms it will find sympathetic. In reinforcing stereotypes of devout Muslims as fundamentalists that are already inscribed in the media, his work offers little prospect of any kind of constructive dialogue between polarized communities or indeed within Muslim communities.

Kureishi's creative focus on British Asian Muslims appears to stem from a desire to 'explain' the contemporary resurgence of Islam in Britain. In the preface to *My Son*, Kureishi emphasizes the causal connection between white racism, separatism and Muslim militancy: 'Muslim fundamentalism has always seemed to me to be profoundly wrong, unnecessarily restrictive and frequently cruel. But there are reasons for its revival that are comprehensible . . . it is constraining, limiting, degrading, to be a victim in your own country. If you feel excluded it might be tempting to exclude others' (MSF pp. xii, xi). *Black Album* and *My Son* are fictional responses to issues raised by Ayatollah Khomeini's death threat to Rushdie (Kureishi's close friend and mentor) and the calls to ban *The Satanic Verses* in 1989. However, Kureishi's anxieties about separatism and Islamic fundamentalism date back to his early essays 'The Rainbow Sign' (1986) and 'Bradford' (1986). In 'The Rainbow Sign', Kureishi explains the revival of Islam in its diasporic forms in loaded terms: as a 'symptom of extreme alienation', but also as an *'aberration'* (*MBL* 79; emphasis mine).[8] He describes separatism, though 'spawned by racism', as a *'pathetic elevation* of an imaginary homeland' (*MBL* 94; emphasis mine).

Despite his sympathy regarding the conditions that heighten Islamic fundamentalism, Kureishi never questions the assumptions and biases of liberal ideology nor the limits of liberalism in accommodating minorities in pluralistic societies. He does not engage with the possibility of a rethinking of liberal ideology. In 'The Rainbow Sign' Kureishi asserts that it is the dominant values of the majority community that need to be problematized and transformed, rather than patronizing toleration:

> In the meantime it must be made clear that blacks don't require 'tolerance' in this particular condescending way. It isn't this particular paternal tyranny that is wanted, since it is major adjustments to British society that have to be made.
> I stress that it is the . . . white . . . British who have to make these adjustments. . . . This decision is not one about a small group of irrelevant people who can be contemptuously described as 'minorities'. It is about the direction of British society. (*MBL* 101–2)

(Kureishi's exact meaning is opaque. He suggests what is required of the majority community is not tolerance, but he does not expand on the nature of these 'adjustments'.) However, ultimately Kureishi's liberalism is close to its hegemonic forms: a form of co-optive liberal pluralism that involves the 'extension of established values and protections over the formerly excluded group, either a liberal bringing into or a Habermasian collectivist extension of the status quo'.[9] But this model does not work with Islam.[10] Kureishi's work embodies a canonically liberal position: intolerance of any intolerance of itself. It also lays bare the problem facing various modes of liberal multi-culturalism which espouse freedom to pursue one's own beliefs and self-interest, and so then must allow that in others, but the liberal dilemma occurs when these beliefs clash with those of the host society.[11] Kureishi does not appear bothered by this contradiction in liberalism. He unselfconsciously rehearses it without unpacking it. For example, echoing Rushdie's work, Shahid concludes towards the end of *Black Album*: 'There had to be innumerable ways of being in the world', but, as we will see, the text does not extend this liberal tolerance to all (*BA* 274).

THE BLACK ALBUM: LIBERAL OR LIBERTARIAN?

Five years on from *Buddha*, Kureishi creates another young British Asian, Shahid Hassan, who escapes suburban Kent for a life in London as a student in 1989. Characteristically, London in the late eighties is powerfully evoked in all its amorphous squalor and limitless possibilities. Shahid is eager to learn, and to experience the pleasures of his new city and to 'slough' off his former life and self (*BA* 190). Once again, the first-person narrator's coming of age is dramatized within a loose picaresque form. Shahid is confronted with different choices from those of his precursors. The novel explores the conflict between funda-mentalism and a form of liberal individualism that is bound up with sensual gratification. The choice is personified somewhat schematically between Shahid's Asian neighbour, Riaz, a mature student and stern leader of the young Muslims at Shahid's derelict North London college, and his white, liberal ex-hippie tutor Deedee Osgood who offers him sex, raves, Ecstasy and postmodern uncertainties. She is a rather caricatured figure of white feminized sexual hedonism. The insistent juxtaposition between Shahid's sexual life with Deedee and his encounter with the 'rave' scene of 1989, and the Islamic group 'forbidden to kiss or touch' is overdone (*BA* 126). Shahid wavers between intimacy and sexual experimentation with Deedee and helping in anti-racist vigils and typing Riaz's religious tracts. Finally, the Muslim students burn a copy of Salman Rushdie's *The Satanic Verses* on campus, which precipitates his decision to leave the group.

Deedee speaks out against the book-burning and calls the police. The group plan to teach her a 'lesson', when they discover Shahid's own act of blasphemy in rewriting Riaz's religious writings as an erotic epic. Chad (Riaz's henchman) and Sadiq assault Shahid for having 'deceived and spat on his own people' (*BA* 266). At the last moment, Shahid's wastrel brother Chilli (a familiar Kureishi creation, a brash, materialistic arch-Thatcherite) saves Shahid and ejects the posse. The group moves on to 'other business', Chad is badly burnt by firebombing a bookshop that sells *The Satanic Verses*. The novel ends with Shahid and Deedee escaping the aftermath of the book-burning and firebombing on a weekend trip to the countryside 'until it stops being fun' (*BA* 276).

Once again, passion wins over politics. Shahid and Deedee's affair eclipses the turbulence around them, underscoring Kureishi's accumulative or incremental privileging of political disengagement. In *Buddha* Karim's evasion of political commitment is at least partially satirized. In contrast, in this novel the 'debate' is so weighted against the Islamists that Shahid's liberal individualism and decision to leave the 'paranoid' Islamic group is unequivocally presented as enlightened self-interest (*BA* 258). If, as I have suggested, Kureishi's *Sammy and Rose* and *Buddha* are 'dialogic', making the reader provide the closure, in contrast this later text is 'monologic', less complex and nuanced and therefore weaker. This is reflected in the novel's form: while *Black Album* is scattered with multiple perspectives and myriad subplots (such as the discovery of a divinely inscribed aubergine), they all appear to be marshalled in order to articulate the novel's central conflict.

Black Album presents Shahid's 'choice' in political terms between polarities of liberalism and Islamic fundamentalism. However, like Kureishi's other male protagonists, Shahid is concerned with the more nebulous aspects of 'this matter of belonging' to a religious and ethnic community, and to Britain, as well as to his lover and family (*BA* 175). In a manner now characteristic of the Kureishi hero, Shahid is equivocal about belonging to 'his people'. Shahid is initially attracted to the group of Muslim students at college out of loneliness and because, 'These days everyone was insisting on their own identity, coming out as a man, woman, black, Jew – brandishing whatever features they could claim...' He fears 'ignorance' about his 'own people would place him in no man's land' (*BA* 92). At first he is drawn to the sense of purpose and belonging created by joining the group: 'He couldn't leave his friends; they had something to fight for; they were his people; he had pledged himself to them' (*BA* 125). Ultimately he finds the group too oppressive and stifling. The problem is not that Shahid is uncertain about belonging to 'his people', but the way Kureishi defines the terms of belonging between extreme polarities of unquestioning solidarity and complete conformity, or total rejection. We will return to the opposition Kureishi sets up between the individual and the communal. Shahid finds 'belonging' or commitment on a personal level equally difficult. He veers between desire for Deedee and fear of 'what this woman might want or expect from him, the demands she might make, the emotion she might feel, and induce him to feel' and resents her 'confining him' (*BA* 104, 208). Deedee, however, emphasizes the provisionality of their relationship and identities. She introduces Shahid to more fluid, mutable notions of identity. The text briefly engages with the reversal of gender roles in a cross-dressing experiment. These more intangible concerns surface, but are not explored in much depth in this schematic novel where, for example, this fluidity is implicitly defined against the 'ecstatic rigidity' of the 'fundamentalists' (*BA* 225). Kureishi's later work *Intimacy* explores the ambivalence of 'belonging' more fully.

Let's first look at Kureishi's exploration of the causes of the resurgence of Islam amongst second-generation Asians in *Black Album* and then examine his portrayals of the Islamic group. In this novel, he begins by presenting the Muslim students' militancy not as an 'aberration' but as a concrete response to racial aggression. One of the most powerful scenes of the novel depicts the Muslim students' all-night vigilante patrol to protect an Asian family living in fear of further racial attacks in a run-down, racist housing estate in London's East End. The text also emphasizes the way 'Fundamentalism provides security' (*MSF* p. xii) and the assertion of an Islamic identity as a positive identity for Asian youth. As former druggie Chad insists, 'No more Paki. Me a Muslim' (*BA* 128).

Black Album implicitly suggests that the drive towards fundamentalism is not simply a response to exclusion, but is equally motivated by a desire to possess a more clearly defined identity. This is explicitly articulated in *My Son*, albeit in a somewhat clichéd way. Quasi-liberal Parvez insists integration is the only possible option: 'Anyhow, how else can we belong here except by mixing up all altogether?'(*MSF* 65). His fundamentalist son Farid's response hints that the impulse towards fundamentalism and separatism stems from anxieties over blurred identities:

> Farid: Can you put keema with strawberries? In the end our cultures...they cannot be mixed.
> Parvez: Everything is mingling already together, this thing and the other!
> Farid: Some of us are wanting something more besides muddle. (*MSF* 39)

Kureishi is clearly influenced by Rushdie, who is opposed to those uncomfortable with hybridized identities and 'of the opinion that intermingling with different cultures will inevitably weaken and ruin their own.'[12] Kureishi's writing appears broadly to endorse Rushdie's celebration of cultural hybridity, 'impurity' and 'intermingling' and his promotion of the liberal value of multicultural hybridization. At the same time, neither author glosses over the diverse modalities of hybridity: 'forced assimilation, internalized self-rejection, political co-optation, social conformism, cultural mimicry and creative transcendence'.[13] Consequently, as in Rushdie's *The Satanic Verses*, Kureishi's complex characterizations embodying the disabling and unstable aspects of cultural hybridity stand in uneasy relation to articulations in his fiction and non-fiction that tend towards generalizing celebrations of hybridity.[14] Kureishi's creations can be usefully read against Homi Bhabha's influential theorizing of cultural hybridity.[15] In *Black Album*, a character emerges from the interstices of society for whom Homi Bhabha's optimistic evocation of enabling or empowering hybridity rings hollow: Chad's 'soul got lost in translation.'(*BA* 107).[16] Adopted by a white couple Chad felt excluded from 'ordinary English people who were secure, who effortlessly belonged. ...When he got to be a teenager he saw he had no roots, no connection with

Pakistan, couldn't even speak the language. So he went to Urdu classes. But when he tried asking for the salt in Southall everyone fell about at his accent' (*BA* 106–7).

However, despite Kureishi's sympathy for his characters' cultural disorientation, the attempt to demonstrate the draw of Islam for young people fails. His commitment to a liberal schema and individualism is such that (as he himself observes) he remains 'perplexed' as to why 'young people, brought up in secular Britain, would turn to a form of belief that denied them the pleasures of the society in which they lived' (*MSF*, p. vii). This may explain why his characterizations of the 'fundamentalists' remain unpersuasive. As the *Financial Times* review of *Black Album* notes: 'Kureishi is far more convincing when writing about Shahid's introduction to heavy drugs than about induction into heavy religion. The passages detailing the growing organisation and fundamentalism of the Moslem student group have a halting, dream-like quality'.[17] Given his vaunted position on the radical fringes of London's urban culture, Kureishi is singularly ill equipped to give insight into a group which decries the lifestyle he cherishes.

In view of Kureishi's own fictional portrayals of British Muslims, his critique of the 'tendentious' images of Islam in the media is ironic (*MSF* p. ix). Kureishi described his novel as 'about the issues that interested [him] at the time of the *fatwa*'. He states that many British Muslims see the *fatwa* as 'a terrible mistake. It's been very bad propaganda for Islam. It's allowed it to be represented as something it doesn't have to be, with Muslims labelled as fanatics and book-burners'. He argues that to abstain from commentary or critique 'would be a disaster for everyone – including Muslims – if we couldn't write about religion or ourselves. It would be playing into the hands of people who think badly of Islam, who say it's so volatile and insular and intolerant, Muslims will go nuts. Those I've met aren't like that at all'.[18]

In fact, Kureishi intensifies in two ways the very perceptions he claims to want to oppose.[19] First, despite the promise of a more nuanced account, Kureishi *invents* a polarity between Islamic fundamentalism and detached liberal individualism or secularism. Apart from Shahid's family, who scorn religion

(Shahid's father, brother Chilli and Chilli's patrician wife Zulma), all the Muslims in this novel are extreme 'fundamentalists'. Kureishi's polarity ignores the range of different forms of Islam that are not extreme or aggressive. This implicitly positions Islamic beliefs as problematic in themselves and illustrates one of the ways in which practising Muslims are, as Modood claims, demonized and perceived as a 'divisive' identity.[20] We shall return to this point towards the end of this chapter. There is no suggestion that devout Muslims were not unequivocal about either Rushdie or the Ayatollah's *fatwa*.[21] Or that not all of those offended by Rushdie's text supported the *fatwa* or the book-burnings. I am not suggesting that Kureishi distorts 'real' Muslims or fails to provide positive images of a marginalized group, nor am I contesting the idea that there is a repressive strain of Islam that does not allow the possibility of dissent and is as intolerant as Kureishi suggests. My point is that in contrast to *Laundrette*, *Black Album*'s monolithic portrait of the Islamic believers does not articulate a range of heterogeneous voices on its central issues. For example, the endorsement of the *fatwa* is presented as unquestioning: 'The feeling was unanimous. Riaz had informed Chad they were rejoicing on the Ayatollah's action, and Chad had passed this in to the group' (*BA* 169). At the meeting to discuss the *fatwa*, only Shahid speaks for the importance of 'the individual voice' (*BA* 184): 'There was a silence. People sat with averted eyes; it wasn't that they were afraid to speak, they had nothing to say' (*BA* 183). Kureishi's essay 'Bradford' argues it is a vocal sect of Islamic men who give the religion and community an intolerant face and that the community is not unified on issues such as separatism and the position of women (*MBL* 136). However, little indication is given in this novel of the shades of opinion and range of responses within this 'highly diverse and internally conflicted religious community'.[22] This points to the weakness of the novel's schematic structure. Kureishi homogenizes the group because if it is not positioned in virtually monolithic agreement this would undermine the dramatic conflict between liberals and 'fundamentalists' that underpins the book.

Secondly, Kureishi's caricature of the British Muslims conforms to the stereotypes he ostensibly challenges. Kureishi rehearses stereotypes of Muslims as intrinsically violent: Chad is characterized as volatile and 'crazy', all 'bulk and suppressed violence' with 'the ferocity of a wild pig' (BA 78, 237). The posse's political activism soon 'inevitably' descends into extremism – book-burning, the firebombing of shops and assault – and so endorses dominant stereotypes of Islamic opposition. The most violent scene in the text occurs when his former Islamic friends beat up Shahid. As Jaggi observes, Hat is 'the sole dissenting Muslim voice' who apologizes to Shahid for the group assault: 'Whatever you done... only God can... condemn' (BA 271).[23] Thus, despite Kureishi's claims, Black Album does little to counter what Modood describes as 'the blend of anti-Muslim prejudice and colour-racism in the hysterical over-reaction to the anti-Satanic Verses demonstrators [that] brought to the surface a highly specific form of cultural racism', such as 'the denunciation of the demonstrators as Nazis'.[24]

As the opening citation suggests, Kureishi reiterates his impartiality in the portrayal of the Islamic group in Black Album. He suggests Shahid chooses an open-minded 'provisionality': 'He makes an effort to join their community, but he can't fit in'.[25] Nonetheless, Shahid's rejection of Islam is presented as a triumph of rationality and common sense over fanatic anti-intellectualism: 'How narrow they were, how unintelligent, how... embarrassing it all was!... the thought of Riaz now made Shahid shudder in revulsion. What a dull and unctuous man he was; how limited and encased was his mind, how full of spite and acidity!' (BA 225, 240). The schematic nature of the novel is reinforced by Kureishi's style. Instead of allowing the issues to live creatively in the dialogue, the characters function as mouthpieces for conflicting beliefs: democracy and freedom of speech versus authoritarianism and censorship; Shahid's love of literature and his delight in imaginative explorations, pitted against the group's dogmatism and resistance to art.

The dialogues articulating opposing viewpoints in Kureishi's text illustrate the importance of being alert to the dangers of what Shohat and Stam refer to as ' "pseudo-polyphonic" discourse'. This 'marginalizes and disempowers certain voices, then pretends to dialog with a puppet-like entity already maneuvered into crucial compromises. ... Polyphony does not consist in the mere appearance of a representative of a given group but rather in the fostering of a textual setting where the group's voice can be heard with its full force and resonance.'[26] Kureishi makes no effort to talk about Islam, fundamentalism or separatism (already highly charged terms in Britain) except in a caricatured way, sometimes implicitly eliding the desire to adopt distinct cultural values with separatism. The text proliferates binary polarities between anti-intellectualism and the free inquiry of rational Western liberal thought: Riaz exhorts Shahid to 'dismiss questions – Just believe in the truth! These intellectuals tie themselves up in knots' (*BA* 175). Riaz describes their Marxist lecturer Brownlow's attitude to Islam as symptomatic of the 'smug intellectual atmosphere of Western civilisation . . . [and the desire] to dominate others with your particular morality, which has . . . gone hand-in-hand with fascist imperialism' (*BA* 98–9). Yet despite this critique, the text ultimately reinforces the 'superiority' of Western ideologies identified with the freedom of sexual expression and polarized against the 'irrationality' of Islam.

Reviewers tend to reinscribe the clichés in Kureishi's portrayals. The *Daily Express* describes the main objects of satire as the 'politically correct' and the 'ghastly Muslim fundamentalists'.[27] The *Sunday Times* review of *Black Album* refers to the 'scary fanaticism' of British-born Muslims'.[28] One might expect *The Times*'s usually conservative stance on drugs to surface, but even this is jettisoned when hedonism is defined in opposition to what is perceived as even more threatening, fundamentalism. This kind of response underscores the way in which Kureishi is able to exploit a liberal distrust of fundamentalism to privilege hedonism. Critics also reinforce some of the polarities that Kureishi 'produces'. Donald Weber in the *Massachusetts Review* describes Shahid as 'torn between the appeal of religious orthodoxy and the claims of personal imagination'. He rejects 'fanatic anti-intellectualism in the name of the capricious, fluid, playful [read Western] imagination'. Here Kureishi is presented as a subversive crusader against 'uninterrogated religious and cultural pieties'. His 'instinctive impulse to take on the poison of both Thatcherism and Islam' is emphasized and commended. This is an example of a recurrent tendency to interpret Kureishi's work in terms of his own self-conscious presentation. Kureishi as the liberal artist in society, asserting his right to artistic freedom, bravely defying the censoring *'policing* efforts of...worried Pakistani emigrants in London'.[29] The ease with which Kureishi's creative portrayals lend themselves to stereotypes, despite his stated wish 'to be fair' and approach the Muslim fundamentalists with sympathy, indicates the penetration of dominant representations and illustrates that textual complexities cannot be contained within authorial intentions.

'MY SON THE FANATIC' – THE SHORT STORY

This short story (first published in the *New Yorker* in 1994) expands the intergenerational conflict that surfaced in *Black Album*. In contrast to the second generation rebelling against their parents' traditional values in *Borderline* set in the 1970s, *Black Album* depicts second-generation Muslim children who seek to reassert religious traditions and prohibitions their quasi-liberal parents have abandoned. Riaz 'was kicked out of his parents' house for denouncing his own father for drinking alcohol. Riaz further reprimanded him for praying in his armchair and not on his knees' (*BA* 109). This becomes the central conflict in 'My Son the Fanatic'. Ali admonishes his father Parvez for his failure to observe the rules of the Koran and rejects the material possessions that Parvez has worked punishing hours as a taxi-driver to provide for him. Father and son have different views of Britain. For Ali, it is the experience of 'living in this country' with the sinful 'Western materialists' who 'hate us' that has led him to embrace Islam. In contrast, Parvez 'love[s] England' because they 'let you do almost anything here' (*LIBT* 126). He desires only Ali's success to symbolize acceptance by the host community and validate the original decision to emigrate to Britain: 'Was it asking too much for Ali to get a good job now, marry the right girl and start a family? Once this happened...his dreams of doing well in England would have come true' (*LIBT* 120). Kureishi remains fascinated by the irony of the reversal of the traditional parent – versus – rebellious – second-generation paradigm. In contrast to Kureishi's earlier work, where the reader is encouraged to identify with protagonists of the younger generation, in this short story the father Parvez's perspective is privileged. Kureishi adapted his short story into a screenplay. Directed in an intimate, atmospheric style by Udayan Prasad, it featured in Britain in 1998.

MY SON THE FANATIC – THE SCREENPLAY

Although Kureishi's screenplay revolves around the same conflicts as *Black Album*, it is a more complex work and undermines the simplistic dichotomy it sets up. Ultimately the text cannot be contained within the fundamentalist/liberal axis but can be read as a broader critique of patriarchy. *My Son* is set in the northern industrial mill town of Bradford, which has a high concentration of South Asian Muslims. It extends the short story's conflict between the quasi-liberal, westernized Pakistani taxi-driver Parvez (Om Puri), who loves Scotch, jazz and bacon-butties, and his (now named) son Farid's new-found religious zeal. Farid (Akbar Kurtha) abandons his white fiancée, accountancy career, guitar and cricket playing to embrace a fundamentalist sect of Islam. He invites a *maulvi* from Lahore, with whose help the young acolytes launch a demonstration against local sex-workers that erupts into violence. (These wider, escalating tensions provide the momentum necessary for the film medium.) This is further complicated as Parvez has begun a love affair with one of the sex-workers, Bettina (Rachel Griffiths), his confidante over his concerns about Farid. Their unfolding relationship, set against the backdrop of their twilight world on the fringe of society (and scrutinized by the enclosed Asian community), is the strongest part of the film: moving, tender, yet without sentimentality. Farid's assault on Bettina at the demonstration provokes Parvez to lash out at Farid inciting him to leave home. Parvez's wife Minoo (Gopi Desai) – who despite her occasional fiery outbursts remains a stereotype of a traditional, devoted South Asian wife – conveniently leaves for Lahore and Parvez is now free (although the film's conclusion is ambiguous) to pursue (what is always privileged in Kureishi's work) his transgressive, inter-racial relationship with Bettina. In contrast to the short story, the film is centrally concerned with the way Parvez's life is thrown into crisis, which forces him to rethink how he wants to live, and begin anew.

The link between exclusion and Farid's desire to discover his Islamic identity is dramatized more effectively in this filmic text than in *Black Album*. We witness Farid's movement from potential integration (in his engagement to his white girlfriend) to separatism and fundamentalism. The film opens with Farid and his parents at Madeleine's home at a strained celebration of their engagement. The subtle tensions of this scene are superbly realized. Kureishi's ability to distil the seeds of Farid's subsequent transformation into a single vignette is an example of his particular strength as a screenwriter. In the directions, '*Parvez is both terrified and ecstatic to be there*' (*MSF* 3). (Although this is not present in the film, Kureishi's text articulates Parvez's resentment that after 'All the years I've lived here, not one single Englishman has invited me to his house' (*MSF* 65). '*Farid is cringing... embarrassed and repelled*' by both his father's attempts to ingratiate himself with Madeleine's snobbish middle-class parents (police chief Inspector Fingerhut and his wife), and by the latter's thinly veiled contempt and displeasure over the match (*MSF* 6–7). Later Farid refers to this incident when he explains why he broke off his engagement. Farid comments: 'Surely you grasped how ashamed I was, seeing you toadying to Fingerhut. ... Do you think his men care about racial attacks? And couldn't you see how much he hated his daughter being with me, and how repellent... he found you?' Parvez, incredulous and unable to respond, '*stares at him in shock*' (*MSF* 68). In this instance, Farid confronts the insidious forms of racism that his father is prepared to overlook. But, on the whole, the dialogues between the two tend to define Parvez as an enlightened, down-to-earth voice of reason, realistic and humane, in contrast to his deluded, indoctrinated and self-righteous son. Significantly, in his preface, Kureishi insists that the young Islamists he interviewed 'were not stupid; many were very intelligent' (*MSF*, p. viii). Despite this assurance, his 'fundamentalist' Muslim characters never express themselves in anything but clichés, as if to suggest they are simply enunciating internalized propaganda. In Kureishi's screenplay, Farid argues: 'This is the true alternative to empty living from day to day... in the capitalist dominated world we are suffering from!' (*MSF* 69).

Like the short story, the script and characterization work

against Farid. Parvez has the sharpest lines and the primary point of view. The film manipulates spectatorial allegiances to identify with warm, genial Parvez: we see him in a tender affair with Bettina, and his desperate efforts to reach his son. His bewilderment over his son's metamorphosis is poignant; his child-like attempt to disturb the *maulvi* by playing loud pop music is comic and engaging. In contrast, Farid's portrayal is more one-dimensional; moreover he is ungrateful, cold, distant and unfeeling to the people he hurts. Although there is one scene where Farid carries Parvez into the house to prevent his bare feet from getting cold, which suggests a spark of warmth. Unlike *Black Album*, where the 'debate' was heavily weighted against the Islamists, *My Son* does not raise Farid's arguments simply to dismiss them. There is a complex irony in the final confrontation between father and son: there is literal 'truth' in Farid's accusations and yet Parvez's incredulous expression suggests he cannot recognize himself as a 'dirty...pimp who organizes sexual parties' (*MSF* 117). The audience is presented with irreconcilable 'truths'.

In *Black Album* the activities of the 'fundamentalists' were more defensive, albeit in violent protest. In *My Son* white intolerance is portrayed; for example the racist bigotry of the stand-up comic in the scene where Parvez, Bettina and her German client Schitz attend a cabaret. However, it is the Islamists' intolerance that emerges as the most disruptive and destabilizing factor. The violence of the demonstration goes beyond 'an assertion of a Muslim subjectivity to a full-blooded attempt to reconstruct society on Islamic principles', putting 'fundamentalist' principles into practice.[30] During the demon-stration, the sex-workers' base is firebombed and the women are assaulted and spat on. On the one hand, this is a crude example of intolerance rehearsing dominant fears of 'them taking over' in terms of the liberal 'dilemma' of how a 'tolerant society' deals with an 'intolerant' one. On the other hand, in contrast to *Black Album*, the text undermines this polarity of 'violent fundamen-talists' versus 'tolerant liberals'. First, Parvez's assault on Farid is equally extreme and intolerant: as Farid's response makes clear, 'You call me a fanatic, dirty man, but who is the fanatic now?' (*MSF* 117) The scene Kureishi originally scripted, where Parvez attempts to force Minoo to have sex with him, would have further complicated this polarity, broadening the film's critique of patriarchy across the board. However, this scene was censored in the film version.[31] It is significant that, in contrast, the Muslim group's vicious, misogynistic harassment of the sex-workers was not considered too violent or inflammatory. The film does gesture towards other local hostility to the sex-workers, as Parvez explains: 'Local people and religious types don't like. Condom and all, you know, hanging from rosebushes (*MSF* 11). The articulation of dissension within the mosque undoes monolithic conceptions of the religious community. One older member voices the intergenerational conflicts within the mosque and the elders' ambivalent response to the younger group:

> These boys are not welcome. They are always arguing with the elders. They think everyone but them is corrupt and foolish. ... They are always fighting for radical actions on many subjects. It is irritating us all here, yaar. But they have something these young people – they're not afraid of the truth. They stand up for things. We never did that. (*MSF* 58)

In the scene depicting the preparations for the demonstration, the *maulvi* instructs the boys that there should be 'no violence'. This is not in the original script and is inserted perhaps to suggest the violence was spontaneous and not planned by the *maulvi*. At the same time, Kureishi appears more sympathetic to the young acolytes, portrayed as misguided youth who, however 'deluded', believed in what they were doing, than to the *maulvi*. He is made to look superficial, for instance in his rapt attention to a children's cartoon. He is portrayed as a hypocrite who stereotypes the West as steeped in filth (ignoring Parvez's observation that 'The wild spice and variety of life is goes on everywhere – like in Lahore, and Karachi. Eh?' (*MSF* 83), and yet wants to 'stay in this immoral country' (*MSF* 109).

This work is more nuanced than *Black Album* in that the critique of Muslim men is part of a wider indictment of patriarchal abuse. The misogyny of the Muslim men's brutal harassment of the sex-workers is targeted. The women accuse the Islamists of beating up a 15-year-old member of their group, although Farid denies this. Patriarchal double standards are explored in the hypocrisy of Parvez's fellow taxi-driver Rashid (not one of the fundamentalist group), previously seen (in the original script) groping the women, who then assaults one of them during the demonstration. The film engages only super-ficially with the oppression of women within the Muslim community: patriarchal attitudes are alluded to in Farid's comment: 'Many [women] lack belief, and therefore rea-son'(*MSF* 69). The gender segregation in their home after the *maulvi*'s visit is an example highlighted by many reviewers. In reviewer's shorthand, the *Financial Times* focuses on the impact of the *maulvi*'s visit: 'messianic misogyny bans mum to the kitchen' and ignores Kureishi's more subtle, ambivalent take on this.[32] The directions portray the previously isolated Minoo with *'young women in the hijab cooking for the troops outside... in a comfortable chair, with her feet up, chats to the women, enjoying their company, and the hustle and bustle'* (*MSF* 106). Another scene makes the significant point that Minoo has not benefited from her husband's westernization: 'If I'd been given your free-dom... think what I would have done... I would have studied. I would have gone everywhere. And talked... talked' (*MSF* 23–4). This is not present in the film version. This suggests that some of the complexity of Kureishi's script is lost in the adaptation.

Rather than limit himself to the liberalism/fundamentalism debate, in *My Son*, Kureishi seems to be interested in examining the sex-workers as an ambivalent site of female exploitation and empowerment, although it is the former that is most convincing. The portrayals of the male clients are trenchant critiques of forms of masculinity. The scenes are explicit and searing. Through Parvez's car mirror we see Bettina's expressionless face beyond disgust while a client reaches orgasm. Bettina is portrayed as defiant and unafraid of her client Schitz, she verbally challenges the way he crudely objectifies her, but the bruises on her back tell another story. Characteristically, Kureishi neither sentimentalizes nor victimizes the women. In the scene of the 'sexual' party Schitz organizes with Parvez's help, Kureishi's directions underline his concern to suggest the shifting power dynamics in these kinds of encounters: *'The two Strippers start trying to undress the Men. One Sikh Businessman has his shirt off and his trousers down. Another man is resisting, as the Stripper sits on his chest and tries pulling his shirt off. The unselfconscious women seem to attack the Men, pulling at them, humiliating them'* (*MSF* 100). This element is not foregrounded in the film version. This idea is explicitly examined and stems from Kureishi's earlier essay 'Wild Women, Wild Men', a factual account of Zarina and Qumar who made money as 'Pakistani Muslims who stripped and did a lesbian double-act' (*MBL* 147). Kureishi emphasizes the 'anarchic' element of their show. He observes, though the Asian male audience came to see the women, part of the act was to round on the men, 'not to turn them on – to humiliate them and frighten them' (*MBL* 150). Altogether, the density and complexity of *My Son* spills over its own frame, making this a richer work than *Black Album*.

In *Black Album* we learn that the college principal had 'long been suspicious of Riaz's group, but, afraid of accusations of racism, she'd secured them a prayer room and otherwise avoided them, even when their posters were inflammatory' (*BA* 226). Here the novel suggests that fear of such accusations can lead to abstention from any form of critique. At one level this is a self-conscious construction of Kureishi's defiance of such censoring impulses; at the same time his work on British Muslims and my response raise an inevitable and important question. Is it possible to question the oppressive aspects of fundamentalism – most pertinently the way it is used to assert patriarchal authority and misogyny without accusations of Eurocentrism or endorsing racist stereotypes?

In this context I want to examine Bhabha's essay 'Unpacking my library...again', which is aligned in some respects to Kureishi's critique of fundamentalism, but points towards the possibility of a more nuanced examination and approach. Like Kureishi, Bhabha opposes the way fundamentalism 'limits choice to a pre-given authority or a protocol of precedence and tradition'.[33] However, in contrast, Bhabha also alerts us to the limits of liberalism as evidenced in some liberal responses to fundamentalism that emerged in the wake of the Rushdie Affair. Bhabha observes that the 'trouble with concepts like individualism, liberalism or secularism' is that 'they seem "natural" to us: it is as if they are instinctive to our sense of what civil society or civil consciousness must be'.[34] Bhabha cautions against such use of the term 'liberalism' as 'natural'. He suggests that it is the 'complex, self-contradictory history of "universal" concepts like liberalism, *transformed through their colonial and post-colonial contexts,* that are particularly important to our current social and cultural debates in a multicultural and multi-ethnic society'. Signalling the dangers implicit in the opposition between fundamentalism and traditional notions of 'secularism', Bhabha unpacks such constructions of secularism, suggesting they can be imperialistic. He reveals the abuse of the term '"secularism"... by many spokespersons of the Eurocentric liberal "arts" establishment who have used it to characterise the "backwardness" of migrant communities in the post-*Satanic Verses* cataclysm. Great care must be taken to "separate" secularism from the unquestioned adherence to a kind of ethnocentric and Eurocentric belief in the self-proclaimed values of *modernisation'.* Bhabha argues that the traditional claim to secularism is based on an 'unreconstructed liberalism' that presupposes an even playing field, a utopian notion of the self as sovereign and '"free" choice as inherent in the individual.' This bears no relation to the marginalized. Such a 'secularism of the privileged' is differentiated from the secularism claimed by minority groups who struggle against inequities of race, class, gender or generation. Injustices 'exerted by state institutions against minority groups, or by patriarchal and *class* structures within minority communities themselves'.[35]

Kureishi's observations on an Islamic school exclusively for girls (which restricts their education to a narrow range of subjects and creation theories in science) he visited in Bradford in 1986, illustrates Bhabha's point about the inadequacy of unreconstructed liberalism. As Kureishi makes clear, for these female pupils' 'choice' is not simply individual but conditioned by the patriarchal religious structures within the community:

> But Islamic schools like the one in Bately appeared to violate the principles of a liberal education, and the very ideas to which the school owed its existence. And because of the community's religious beliefs, so important to its members, the future prospects for the girls were reduced. Was that the choice they had made? Did the Asian community really want this kind of separate education anyway? And if it did, how many wanted it? Or was it only a few earnest and repressed believers, all men, frightened of England and their daughters' sexuality. ('Bradford' 133)[36]

Where Kureishi implicitly posits an unreconstructed secularism as an alternative to the way Islamic fundamentalists use religion to assert control over women, for Bhabha, these kinds of oppression evidence the need to assert a redefined, 'subaltern' secularism, an ethical freedom of choice. This 'emerges from the limitations of "liberal" secularism and *keeps faith* with those communities and individuals who have been...excluded from the egalitarian and tolerant values of liberal individualism'.[37]

Furthermore, as I have argued, Kureishi never explores any forms of Islam that are not 'fundamentalist'. His rigidly dualistic approach reinforces what Modood describes as the assumption that 'religion divides, the secular unites...religion is "backward" and negative, secularism is progressive; religious people are the problem and secular rule is the solution'.[38] In contrast, reading Bhabha and Kureishi against each other, we see how Bhabha avoids this trap. Bhabha suggests that 'we need to "secularise" the public sphere so that, paradoxically, we may be free to follow our strange gods or pursue our much-maligned monsters, as part of a collective and collaborative "ethics" of choice'.[39]

Similarly, in his work on British Muslims, Kureishi sets up an irresolvable opposition between community and individual: there is no representation of the communal that is not fundamentalist. Again, Bhabha shows us a way of thinking outside this dichotomy, drawing on Gita Sahgal's articulation of *Women Against Fundamentalism* as an 'emergent secular community'. Sahgal conceives of the space of the women's centre as a secular space 'to practice religion as well as challenge it'. She makes an important point that does not seem to occur to Kureishi: individuals opposed to fundamentalism can still be religious. Sahgal's secular space is an example of how secular choice, 'an ethical freedom of choice', can be communal without being fundamentalist. So, where Kureishi positions the communal in opposition to the individual, Bhabha tries to maintain a notion of secularism that is communal. For Bhabha, 'freedom is much more about the testing of boundaries and limits as part of a *communal collective* process, so that "choice" is less an individualistic desire than it is a public demand and *duty*'.[40]

Finally, Kureishi examines fundamentalism from a liberal perspective. As he emphasizes, he was not brought up with a Muslim background and does not provide a critique from first-hand experience. Kureishi is right to reject this role of spokes-

100

person. These texts undermine his construction by critics as an 'objective' insider/outsider and cultural translator. This is reinforced in his essay 'Bradford' and his preface to *My Son*. Both read like journalistic, anthropological surveys of these 'Other' communities. Kureishi's earlier portrayals engendered intense, engaged responses from members of Britain's black communities and from influential black critics in North America. Significantly, in contrast, his recent work on British Muslims received enthusiastic reviews from several black critics such as Kwame Anthony Appiah, who describes Kureishi's portrayal of the British Pakistanis as 'compassionate and *illuminating*'.[41] This may be because 'fundamentalism' is such a fraught subject and because the stereotypes Kureishi reinscribes are so entrenched in popular conceptions of Muslims, which makes it all the more necessary to contest them.

101

5

Mid-life Crisis – Variations on a Theme

> I suppose I want to be loyal to something else now. Or someone else. Yes; myself. (*I* 32).

Kureishi's recent work marks a break from explorations of race. As we have seen, he first attempts this move in his screenplay *London Kills Me* (1991), but achieved greater success in his recent fictional narratives. *Love in a Blue Time* (1997) embodies his transition. Only three stories in this collection examine the lives of minorities in Britain: 'My Son the Fanatic', 'With your tongue down my throat' – sketches the relationship between two Pakistani/British half-sisters who meet for the first time – and 'We're not Jews' which looks at racism through the eyes of a mixed-race child. The remaining stories in this collection, those in *Midnight All Day* (1999), his novella *Intimacy* (1998) and his play *Sleep With Me* (1999), all explore private forms of masculinity and centre on the theme of mid-life crisis compounded by deteriorating relationships that has of late consumed Kureishi. When first advised to write about growing up as Other in Britain, Kureishi recalls: 'it came to me as an... epiphany this material is rich'.[1] Since then his interests have become increasingly 'universal'. After the publication of *Love in a Blue Time* he suggests his subject at present is 'what it is like to be a human being'.[2] Commenting on the pitfalls of endlessly re-writing one's own experiences and the importance of renewing oneself and developing as a writer, he observes, 'I want to extend my range of writing, because it is interesting for me to find new subjects to write about'. Kureishi clearly takes a delight in broadening his range to include 'quintessentially' English people and settings that were once considered the preserve of white authors. He describes *Sleep With Me* as 'set in the English countryside, and it's got French windows. And it's

102

set in an English country house. And all the characters are white and English. And they're sort of trotting around in this beautiful house. And that amuses me very much *as an Indian*, writing about that'. Kureishi has always insisted on his right to examine wider society: 'I want to feel free to not only be an Asian writer' but 'a writer who is also Asian'.[3] The difficulties in achieving this aim become apparent in the way critics, foreground racial issues in Kureishi's work as paramount. It is not only black critics who impose this requirement to discuss race. Reviews of *Love in a Blue Time* frequently single out for praise the stories that deal with race: 'only the stories which relate personal dilemmas to the larger contexts of race achieve a choked, baffled power'.[4] Similarly a review favourably contrasts Kureishi's autobiographical essay 'The Rainbow Sign', for its 'elliptical brilliance about being at once English and Asian', with *The Buddha of Suburbia* where 'such challenging topics bob tantalizingly into view...and as quickly vanish'.[5]

Kureishi's move from wider explorations of race and class, towards these first-person 'confessional' narratives, recalls central earlier ambivalences and marks a more explicit treatment of themes that surfaced in his previous plays, novels and films: assertions of autonomy in the face of competing commitments to others. His early protagonists are all autonomous individualists. In their narratives, obligations to the group clash with individual freedoms. Similarly, in his more recent work, Kureishi's male protagonists, stifled by long-term relationships and domestic responsibility, wrestle (albeit briefly) with the conflicting claims of autonomy, desire, family and duty. These later confessionals make the concern with individualism a structural principle, most evidently in *Intimacy*, where the narrator Jay broods over his decision to leave his long-term partner and their two young sons. Responsibilities concomitant with the role of father or partner are presented as eroding a sense of self. In these later texts, Kureishi's male protagonists, portrayed as fleeing or preparing to escape from their partners, assert their autonomy by active detachment. This is a recurrent feature of all his writings: the protagonists' resistance to commitment is dramatized by their distancing themselves from the group, whether it is the parental home or 'ethnic' community, collective forms of political action or, now that his protagonists approach middle age, their own family.

Kureishi's recent work centrally explores the tensions between fidelity to self and loyalty to others. The competing claims of happiness and personal sacrifice were first elaborated in *Buddha*. Haroon Amir's infidelity and decision to leave Margaret is sketched with subtlety, complexity and a characteristic ambivalence which stems partly from Karim's perception of how Haroon's actions affect his mother. On the one hand, Karim thinks that 'divorce wasn't something that would occur to them. In the suburbs people rarely dreamed of striking out for happiness. It was all familiarity and endurance: security and safety were the rewards of dullness' (*BS* 8). Haroon and Eva's relationship is shown as mutually fulfilling and beneficial, in contrast to Haroon and Margaret's empty marriage. On the other hand, Karim perceives Haroon's affair as 'serious betrayal, lying, deceit and heart-following' (*BS* 253). Haroon and Eva's mutual passion is also presented as a 'high-spirited egotism-à-deux', a 'narrow-eyed, exclusive, selfish bastard, to enjoy itself at the expense of a woman who now lay in bed in Auntie Jean's house, her life unconsidered' (*BS* 116). When Haroon pontificates, 'Our lives become stale, they become set. We are afraid of the new, of anything that might make us grow or change', Karim dismisses this 'vague and meaningless ... hot air' as selfish rationalizations that do not take into account the 'people around them' (*BS* 89–90). In this way *Buddha* juggles conflicting views. In *My Son the Fanatic*, Parvez is thrown into a similar moral and familial crisis. His passionate affair with Bettina transforms his previously dutiful, routine family-oriented life with which he is no longer satisfied. From this confusion Parvez comes to an understanding of how he wants to live. Bettina and Parvez's intimacy is juxtaposed with his mechanical and distant relationship with Minoo. He stands accused by Minoo of 'one unforgivable thing': putting 'self before family' (*MSF* 121). His poignant response to his boyhood friend Fizzy's remonstrations evokes his dilemma:

> 'What else is there for me, yaar, but sitting behind the wheel without tenderness? That's it for me, is it, until I drop dead, and not another human touch. You are too certain of what everyone else should do! Minoo has never given me satisfaction. Who am I satisfying? You? (*MSF* 112)

It is this resistance to living according to the expectations of others rather than to one's own 'satisfaction' that preoccupies Kureishi.

The male absconders who people Kureishi's later texts recall their precursors in many ways. Like Omar, Haroon Amir, Shahid and Parvez, their assertion of autonomy is often bound up with the pursuit of a new, transgressive relationship defined in different ways against the dominant culture. Moreover, they also find it easier to form new unconventional bonds than face responsibilities. Kureishi's liberated female characters equally favour freely formed, provisional relationships. But on the whole it is his male protagonists who resist political commitment, solidarity and now domestic responsibility. As we have seen, Kureishi's ironic distance renders his stance on this resistance characteristically ambivalent. Haroon (from *Borderline*) and Karim's lack of political commitment is both critiqued and legitimized, although Kureishi accumulatively privileges disengagement and individualism. This new work appears to retrace this trend, characteristically avoiding judgement or clear-cut conclusions. This chapter examines *Love in a Blue Time*'s implicit articulation of the difficulty of balancing a sense of self with commitment to others and *Intimacy*'s dramatization of the interplay between feelings and obligations. Kureishi's texts privilege freely formed relationships that in turn can be freely jettisoned, leaving many of his characters anxious about being left. This is a concern of Kureishi's most recent collection of short stories *Midnight All Day*, although its mood is lighter than either the sexual nihilism and pessimism of *Love in a Blue Time*, or the melancholic ruminations of *Intimacy*.

While these later narratives explore concerns elaborated in his previous work, they mark Kureishi's adoption of a new aesthetic: a different focus, style and tone. In this recent cluster of well-observed stories, he does not attempt epic themes, but brings into intense and startling focus the tumultuous drama of the domestic. From the broad canvas of panoramic, picaresque novels, Kureishi narrows his focus inwards, to explore male interiority. (As a consequence perhaps, although he still recreates seedy, down-at-heel London settings, as well as increasingly more affluent milieus, this work is less anchored in a particular time and place.) Some stories are closer to dramatic monologues than fiction. Kureishi's move towards a confessional narrative is most apparent in *Intimacy*. It was only in the writing of *Intimacy* that he began to explore the 'older, greater interest in inner lives' and exploit to the full the novel, 'the best form, the world's deepest form'. As Kureishi observes wryly, 'in *The Buddha of Suburbia*, I was more interested in what people were wearing'.[6] Now, he explores what he touched on in *Buddha* and *Black Album*: what people are feeling and what constitutes masculinity from the inside. The outwardly focused macho posturing is replaced by the more sustained introspection of self-absorbed male internal monologues, reminiscent of Hardy's *Jude the Obscure* and D. H. Lawrence's novels. Kureishi lays bare private vicious forms of masculinity with lacerating directness in *Intimacy*, where he takes you inside the mind of his protagonist with an alienating effect. The title also refers to the experience of reading the text: none of his previous works expose a character to this extent, nor position the reader inside a character in this way. Although the narrator estranges the reader, Kureishi makes his soliloquy of reflective introspection (relieved by ironic insights) compelling and seductive reading. In this way the text and the experience of reading it enact its subject, the contradictions of intimacy.

This new work shows his ability to delineate contemporary relationships in crisis in a lucid, taut, precise and elegant prose, although the clipped utterances are shorn of the quirky elements that characterized his previous dialogues. The move from novels to the more compressed form of the short story and novella has created a new, more disciplined prose style. (In the latter half of *Buddha* the loose, picaresque narrative loses momentum, direction and drive with the move to the city and to New York. *Black Album* is marked by a lack of narrative structure and focus, flitting from flashback to the present and between several plots.) Kureishi describes the challenge of a short story as a 'great opportunity to capture a moment of life which seems an important epiphany'.[7] His stories are vignettes revolving around enigmatic moments when the characters realize the extent of their frustration and disappointment and fear that 'it was already too late' to achieve their ambitions (*LIBT* 58). In some stories, he develops central images and symbols to convey his theme. *Intimacy*, a novella of only about a hundred pages, reveals a prose style of greater clarity and intensity, sometimes bordering on the claustrophobic. The breathtakingly intense impact of *Intimacy* is heightened because it is compressed over the 'saddest' night before Jay leaves his family. It is *Love in a Blue Time* that first signalled Kureishi's new tone.

LOVE IN A BLUE TIME (1997)

This collection of meditative reflections on disintegrating long-term relationships and the weary desperation of the mid-life crisis contrast sharply with the buoyant prose of Kureishi's previous high-spirited, youthful, lively rites-of-passage narratives. The sharp, satiric eye on vanity and immaturity remains, but the amused observations have given way to pitiless characterization and bleak humour. 'When I was younger', says Kureishi, 'the world seemed a much funnier place'.[8] Sex and drugs are now addictive and compulsive, replacing the liberating youthful desire of his previous work. In contrast to the randy, cheerful protagonists of the earlier erotic movies and raunchy novels, who discover the pleasures of physical and emotional intimacy with relish, many encounters are sordid and impersonal, emphasizing disconnection and the fear of communication. 'Nightlight' depicts an isolated, divorced man whose only contact with the outside world is weekly meetings with a woman he once interviewed for a job when they have sex without speaking. All his life he has been seeking uncomplicated sex, and 'now he has it, it doesn't seem sufficient' (*LIBT* 145). Sex has become darker and violent, men hitting their girlfriends when they reach orgasm. In 'D'accord, Baby', Bill takes revenge on his wife's lover by sleeping with his daughter who wants him to hit her because she 'deserves' it (*LIBT* 59). The protagonists approach middle age, now weighted with responsibility and sometimes parenthood. They are largely failed, unfulfilled men in the media: TV scriptwriters, commercial directors and photographers, who have lost their youthful idealism and prostrated their art, or are 'tormented' by their 'mediocrity' (*LIBT* 17). Kureishi reveals their feelings of under-achievement and search for elusive happiness. It is hard to care about his self-absorbed, angst-ridden and indulgent characters that, in contrast to their precursors, seem somewhat interchangeable.

The tensions and struggles of long-term relationships form the main preoccupation: 'The worst marriages', one character muses 'aren't the most violent or stifling' but 'the ones that are just wrong. People stay because it takes ten years to realise it' (*LIBT* 169–70). Marriage is 'insufficient to satisfy most human need' (*LIBT* 54) so divorce and adultery abound in Kureishi's 'city of love vampires' (*LIBT* 142). Kureishi depicts a generation of men unprepared to relinquish adolescent dreams of freedom, yet confused as to how their lives turned out this way: 'people who'd thought that leaving home was something you did only once' (*LIBT* 142). In 'In a Blue Time' Roy revisits his youthful fascination with escape. He 'thought of the books which had spoken to him as a teenager and how concerned they were with young men fleeing home and domesticity, to hurl themselves at different boundaries. But where had it led except to self-destruction and madness? And how could you do that kind of thing now? Where could you run?' (*LIBT* 22). This story ends with the male character attempting to confront his familial responsibilities. The others tend to feature men 'running' from their partners, 'turning from person to person, hunting the one who will make the difference' (*LIBT* 142). One story rationalizes other people's advice to stay together as moral policing: 'Other people wanted you to live lives as miserable as theirs. This they considered moral behaviour' (*LIBT* 176). This argument resurfaces in *Intimacy*. It is Baxter's dawning realization of the hatred he feels towards the mother of his child in 'The Flies' (a surreal, absurdist tale that portrays the death of marriages as a widespread infestation of insects) that most explicitly anticipates *Intimacy*. Baxter oscillates between desire for his lover and duty to his wife; it 'has all rushed back, what he owes her: kindness, succour, and something else, the details elude him' (*LIBT* 201). These tensions are fleshed out and form the central subject of *Intimacy*, where we see a more self-conscious assertion of self-fulfilment.

INTIMACY (1998)

Jay, a screenwriter, and Susan who works in publishing live in an 'unhappy Eden' (*I* 77) of metropolitan affluence where 'velvet curtains, soft cheese, compelling work and boys who can run full-tilt...isn't enough' (*I* 32). Jay, who we learn has been repeatedly unfaithful, convinced that their relationship is irreparably damaged, and that they 'cannot make one another happy', is on the point of leaving his family (*I* 70). He is 'lost in the middle of [his] life' (*I* 10) and wants to 'become someone else' (*I* 77). In this way the narrative gestures towards an implicit trajectory of the mid-life crisis leading 'inevitably' to infidelity and marital breakdown. Excellent at detail and atmosphere, Kureishi vividly recreates Jay's view of their relationship. Kureishi does not attempt balance, nor is he interested in Susan's perspective. The portrayal of 'deliberate', 'effective' and 'organized' Susan who 'reads cookbooks in bed' is compelling (*I* 22). It is obvious that, however much Jay despised her, he was not indifferent: 'Hurting someone is a reluctant act of intimacy' (*I* 4). Reviewers have read Susan's portrayal as misogynistic, but Jay's unsuccessful attempts to demonize her are crucial to his characterization. Jay's contempt for her 'fat, red weeping' face shows his callousness (*I* 75). As does his now infamous observation: 'there are some fucks for which a person would have their partner and children drown in a freezing sea' (*I* 91). Susan comes across as a far more likeable character. The more he describes her efforts to reach him, and when after all his infidelities he still complains that she 'won't wake up' for him, the more sympathy we feel for her. His relationship with his lover Nina is less convincing. Jay replays their relationship in his mind, wondering if it is love or lust, and by the end he suggests in a passage of inflated prose 'it could only have been love' (*I* 118). The hippie Nina is a shadowy figure of male fantasy. Nina, unlike Susan, is eager to meet all Jay's sexual demands, lets him eat strawberries and cream off her buttocks and likes to 'lie on the floor beside my desk and watch me work' (*I* 67). It is difficult to believe Jay has left Susan because of an 'excess of belief...in the possibilities of...love' (*I* 101).

In *Love in a Blue Time* an ex-husband refers to his children as 'those intermediaries growing up between immovable hatreds

(*LIBT* 139). In contrast to the severance of his relationship with Susan, Jay implies his bond with the children cannot be broken. There is pathos in his awareness that he will miss living with them and that 'She will always know them better than I will' (*I* 89). At the same time, Jay is characteristically ambivalent about his children. He describes his youngest child's 'affectionate words and little voice' as 'God's breath' (*I* 92) and recalls waiting 'for their faces to come through the door, and for the world to be re-animated by their chaotic energy' (*I* 10). Yet, the focus on the children is intermittent, and Jay is hostile to the demands of child-care.

Kureishi's ironic distance makes *Intimacy* ambivalent reading. Read as pure irony, *Intimacy* is a dissection and exposure of Jay's narcissism and self-justification, a satire of selfish, cruel and immature men. Often Jay's self-questioning comes across as rhetorical and superficial. But, as always with Kureishi, his irony is not signalled and not always clearly directed. A purely 'ironical' reading and positioning of Jay as 'villain' is precluded because Jay's controlling perspective is too self-aware. At times he undermines his own rationalizations: 'If one could see one's progress as a kind of experiment, without wishing for an impossible security...some kind of stillness might be attained. You can, of course, experiment with your own life. Maybe you shouldn't do it with other people's' (*I* 38). Jay appears to wrestle with his warring selves, to resist an instinctive disengagement and attempts to break down his own sense of the implacable opposition between freedom and obligations: 'But what am I free for? Surely the ultimate freedom is to choose, to dispense with freedom for the obligations that tie one to life – to get involved' (*I* 11). This brooding mediation dramatizes the interplay between feelings and obligations, and between fidelity to one's own feelings and loyalty to others. Jay assesses his parents' frustrated marriage: 'Nevertheless they were loyal and faithful to one another. Disloyal and unfaithful to themselves. Or do I misunderstand?' (*I* 44). Ultimately Jay concludes that self-betrayal is worse than the betrayal of others, however damaging: 'Tomorrow I will do something that will damage and scar them'(*I* 4). The implication is that if Jay stayed it would be equally destructive; he and Susan would only 'frustrate and punish one another' (*I* 77).

110

However, while he is undermined as self-obsessed, selfish and weak, there is a simultaneous construction of Jay as courageous enough to leave, to defy bourgeois morality, constraints and expectations and to articulate unspeakable truths: 'this is just the way things are'. (This is similar to Kureishi's (self)-construction as 'brave' to critique Pakistanis in Britain.) Kureishi reinforces this interpretation in interviews. He describes *Intimacy* as transgressing the 'Koran of the middle classes'. He interprets *Intimacy*'s hostile reception as a response to its contestation of 'a sacred taboo'. He asserts: 'if you write a book in which a man leaves a woman this is provocative because no one wants to be left. ... It is very important that marriages succeed.' He suggests that 'critics were shooting the messenger'.[9] Once again Kureishi positions his writing at the forefront *contesting* dominant orthodoxies, when he is in actuality reflecting a trend that is on the increase, in Britain at least. In the text, Jay is positioned as part of 'a new restlessness' (*I* 100). This is intensified by Kureishi's claims that his work articulates a new trend: 'Male attitudes to relationships and children are changing'.[10] But how 'new' is it? To what extent is Kureishi's work a justification of 'older' forms of male selfishness, need for freedom and avoidance of commitment, repackaged as 'a new restlessness' and 'new' masculinity?

Kureishi's novella and stories both parody and exonerate his 'privileged and spoilt' derailed generation: the 'inheritors of the freedoms won by our seditious elders in the late sixties' (*I* 53). Kureishi invokes post-sixties freedoms to give a socio-political framework and philosophy for self-indulgence. Defined in contrast to their predecessors, this generation is not constrained by social or religious scruples. Jay declares: 'I am of a generation that believes in the necessity of satisfying oneself' (*I* 60) ... 'All of me, along with the age, stood against compulsion (*I* 69)'. Kureishi defines the contradictions of this generation of 'new' men shaped by feminism and sexual politics. Displaced from the dominant role their fathers occupied, 'where the man had the power and had to be protective' (*I* 43), they are intimidated by female strength and resentful of women's refusal to fulfil all their sexual demands. Nurtured on therapy, psychoanalysis and 'the ungovernable desires of the unconscious' (*I* 74) – 'Freud was our new father, as we turned inwards' (*I* 54) – they are in touch with their feelings to the point of self-obsession. We see flashes of a male backlash against feminists: mocking references to the 'screechings of feminists' and 'she thinks she's a feminist, but she's just bad tempered' (*I* 79). Like his contemporary Nick Hornby (1957–) Kureishi maps relationships between a confused generation of men and their more capable and pragmatic female partners, which may appear to reflect female empowerment, but actually constrains women, 'allowing' their male partners to be wayward and immature. Moreover, in *Intimacy* Susan's capabilities are used to demonize her. In contrast to the gauche heroes of Hornby's comic novels (*Feverpitch*, *High Fidelity*, 1995, and *About A Boy*, 1998), who confess their foibles with self-deprecating wit, Kureishi's acerbic, jaded protagonists seek to alienate and are closer to Martin Amis's anti-heroes. At the same time, Kureishi attempts a more complex exploration than Hornby.

How does Kureishi privilege individualism? Are we allowed to see outside the narrator's controlling perspective and ethos? Jay's stance is defined in relation to two contrary viewpoints. His friend Victor, an ex-husband and 'a recent convert to hedonism', reasserts the former 'radicalism' of his student days, suggesting all those 'barren and arduous nights and years' with his wife were 'blind, foolish obedience and submission' to 'a promise that I had to fulfil at all costs' (*I* 49). Echoing Parvez, who having 'managed to destroy everything...never felt worse...or better' (*MSF* 123), Victor describes leaving his wife and children as 'the worst, and also the best thing I have ever done'. He justifies his decision despite the fact that his devastated sons became fierce, angry and attempted to harm themselves (*I* 102). Jay's other friend Asif articulates an alternative morality. He passionately loves his wife and children and embraces obligations and responsibility. Jay is both envious and dismissive of Asif's 'bourgeois happiness'. Although Kureishi is careful not to make happily married Asif 'worthy' (he admits to being curious as to what another body would feel like), ultimately Asif's disapproval of 'the modern way' implies that he articulates values of an outdated era (*I* 100). There is a suggestion that Asif's serene contentment is possible because he is simple, unlike the complex Jay. Like Asif, Susan advocates what Jay refers to as 'unpleasant' values: 'duty, sacrifice, obligation to others, self-discipline' (*I* 53), but, again contrary to Jay, 'the range of her feelings is narrow' (*I* 23). Defined against Asif and Susan, Jay is constructed as curious, 'yearning for more life' and embracing it (*I* 61).

Kureishi distils the problem of love as the precarious balancing act between involvement and retaining one's sense of self: intersecting not eliding boundaries. In *Intimacy* this difficulty continues into Jay's relationship with Nina. Jay suggests 'you have to find the right distance between people. Too close, they overwhelm you; too far and they abandon you' (*I* 71). Jay fears he may lose Nina if he upsets this equilibrium: 'I overwhelmed her at times. There was too much of me, I know that. We want love but we don't want to lose ourselves' (*I* 95).

Although self-absorbed, this text should not be dismissed as navel-gazing or morose introspection. The glimpses into the male psyche and the portrayal of love disintegrating into consuming hatred provoke recognition however unpalatable. Kureishi's ability to give one couple's failed relationship such resonance gives his work contemporary relevance. He attempts to explore important questions, posed with characteristic mock flippancy. 'Where have all the fathers gone?' Is it when their women become mothers that they flee? (*I* 106) What is it about the mothers that makes it so essential that they be left? (*I* 107). Although he gives a somewhat partial examination of these pressing questions, he offers us an insight into the breaking up of a family from a male perspective, and into the process of rationalization.

Despite the shift from sensitive issues of minority representation, Kureishi continues to court controversy and his construction as *enfant terrible*. A furore erupted over the publication of *Intimacy* because it appeared to be so closely based on his own life: Kureishi left his long-term partner Tracey Scoffield, who worked in publishing, and their twin sons for his younger girlfriend. Scoffield's protest against *Intimacy* was repeatedly quoted in the press: 'Hanif says it's a novel, but nobody believes it's just pure fiction. You might as well call it a fish'.[11] Some of the critics' outrage stemmed from a conflation of text and biography. The blaze of publicity made it virtually impossible to read *Intimacy* in Britain as a work of fiction, although it partly contributed to it becoming a bestseller. Disputes over the collision of fact and fiction and accusations of exploitation continue to dog his career.[12] Just as Gurindher Chadha feels Kureishi used his 'cultural side...without integrity', many feminist critics read *Intimacy* as marital revenge rhetoric.[13] Now Kureishi's masculinist portrayals of Susan have left him open to accusations of misogyny, not internalized racism. Just as *Buddha* thematized the reception of *Laundrette*, Kureishi's subsequent *Midnight All Day* incorporates the controversial reception of *Intimacy* and defends the novel. In the story 'Strangers When We Meet', the protagonist comments: 'I have been reading an account by a contemporary author of his break-up with his partner. It is relentless, and, probably because it rings true, has been taken exception to' (*MAD* 47–8). Similarly, Kureishi thematizes the accusations he faced of exploitation. In 'That Was Then', a woman asks her former lover, 'Why did you take parts of me and put them in a book?' (*MAD* 74). Undeterred, Kureishi's work continues to mine the trajectory of his own life.

SLEEP WITH ME (1999)

A character in Kureishi's ensuing play complains to her husband that 'You don't let me in'; he replies as Jay might: 'You wouldn't like what you saw' (*SWM* 22–3). Kureishi's first play for fifteen years is set over a weekend party in a country house. It sketches the intertwining love lives of a group of friends approaching middle age. *Sleep With Me* recycles much of the material (dialogue, incidents and characters) from *Intimacy* and *LIBT* and re-presents it in a comic, dramatic form. It is closest to *Intimacy*, with a similar egocentric screenwriter, Stephen, who is on the point of leaving his brittle, organized wife and their two young children for his young, uneducated mistress. Stephen has turned his back on the idealism of the sixties and achieved success but is still dissatisfied. Moving away from the intense, internal dramatic monologue of *Intimacy*, Kureishi attempts to broaden his portrait of mid-life crisis by including female perspectives. Stephen's ex-lover Sophie, who abandoned a career in journalism to become a social worker is disillusioned because the gains of feminism that she fought for have made so little impact on her life. She is frustrated with family life and

114

flirts with infidelity. She and her partner Barry, a stereotyped didactic Marxist, envy the lifestyle of their rich friends. The play met a poor critical reception: it was dismissed as a 'trite', 'self-indulgent', thinly veiled rewrite of *Intimacy*.[14]

Having brought concepts of race and sexuality to the fore, redefining minority representations and constructions of contemporary British culture, Kureishi is one of the few writers of Asian origin to have crossed successfully from minority themes to mainstream ones. At the same time, from such an innovative beginning with *Laundrette*, it is disappointing that Kureishi has turned to more standard thematics of male angst and middle-class adultery. Despite its strengths, this recent work has a weary repetitiveness stemming from the relentless reworking of the same theme.

MIDNIGHT ALL DAY (1999)

> People speak of the violence of separation, but what of the delight? (*MAD* 48)

The stories in the collection *Midnight All Day* deal with the consequences of *Intimacy*, describing both the 'violence' and the 'delight' of separation. 'Girl' and 'Four Blue Chairs' articulate its unspoken pleasures in terms of the positive new relationships of older men who, like Kureishi, have left their partners for younger lovers. The collection marks a new stage of comic disavowal. The older lovers are ironized. In 'Four Blue Chairs' John is learning to adapt to his new lover: 'She likes to eat sitting on the front steps in the evening. He is too old for bohemianism, but he can't keep saying "No" to everything, and he has to sit there with pollution going into his bowl of pasta and the neighbours observing him, and men looking at her' (*MAD* 57). The stories register the male characters' sense of panic and pressure to make the relationship work this time.

Invariably it is the men who experience the delights of separation. Kureishi does acknowledge the gendered discrepancy of the impact of separation between mothers and fathers in terms of the different degree of involvement in the upbringing of children, which conditions their future relationships. Although 'Morning in the Bowl of Night' and 'Midnight

All Day' delineate male protagonists struggling to cope with the demands of their children and new lovers, it is the discarded wives' bitterness at their former husbands' new lives and families that is most powerfully evoked in this collection. 'The Umbrella' illustrates the way resentment and furies of ex-partners can erupt over tiny issues. Roger returns the children home from a rainy outing in the park on his way to a date. His estranged wife refuses to lend him an umbrella. This leads to a violent row, with their two sons screaming in the background.

The stories do not gloss over the pain caused by separation. 'Morning in the Bowl of Night' examines with poignancy its fallout on the children. Mikey 'seemed wary and uncertain, as if he weren't sure which parent he should go to, sensing he couldn't favour one without displeasing the other' (*MAD* 201). Mikey pleads with his father to 'stay for ever', to 'kiss mummy' and 'sleep in Mummy's bed'. At the same time, Kureishi seems concerned to represent forms of parenting outside the traditional patterns of marriage or long-term relationships counterpointing divorced fathers and the single mother in 'Sucking Stones'. This is in keeping with his configurations of relationships outside accepted 'norms'.

On balance, this collection has a lighter tone and is more optimistic and upbeat than *Love in a Blue Time* and *Intimacy*. Love remains a precarious struggle with 'each fighting to preserve themselves' (*MAD* 205), but 'without hope, appetite, desire', one character concludes, 'the world was ashes' (*MAD* 203). Kureishi's short story 'Goodbye, Mother', published in *Granta*, continues in this more sanguine vein.[15] The story flits between Harry's past and present and revolves around him taking his troublesome, depressive mother (who haunts him in both the past and present) to visit his father's grave. Harry is sceptical of his partner Alexander's new interest in hypnosis and therapy and mocks her calling it 'work'. As candid but less cruel than *Intimacy*, the text suggests his resistance stems from the fear that 'she was outgrowing him' and that he resents her for changing. He was 'angry that he couldn't control or understand her. By changing she was letting him down; she was leaving him' (*GM* 131). The irony of his resistance to psychoanalysis is that the narrative, in the classic mode of therapy, revisits his childhood (which like Jay's was) blighted by his mother's torpor, enabling him to come to terms with its unresolved conflicts, particularly his resentment of its 'joylessness'. He realizes he is jealous of Alexander's attentions to their daughter because he never experienced such care. He muses, 'It would be childish to blame Mother for what he was now. But if he didn't understand what had happened, he wouldn't be free of his resentment and couldn't move on' (*GM* 121). While Harry is fearful of turning into his mother, the text suggests this awareness may help to prevent him from reproducing the same dynamics in his own family.

APPENDIX: *GABRIEL'S GIFT* (2001)

His most recent novel, *Gabriel's Gift*, reinforces this sense of renewed optimism. Its warmth contrasts sharply with the bitterness of *Intimacy*. This is partly a result of Kureishi's return to a younger narrator. The novel unfolds from 15-year-old Gabriel's point of view, describing his parents' break-up and eventual reunion. Kureishi maintains his interest in the drama of domestic, personal relationships, but in this novel they are refracted through a sympathetic, sensitive adolescent who is both innocent and knowing. This imbues the story with a tenderness that has been missing in Kureishi's recent work. While Gabriel forms a sharp contrast to Kureishi's depressive previous narrators, his insights are sharp and witty, preventing the novel from becoming sentimental.

When the story opens, Gabriel's father has moved out. We learn that in their heyday his parents were part of the seventies rock scene. Now they find themselves outpaced by change. Rex, an unemployed musician, constantly relives his brief moment of fame when he played in a rock band, the 'Leather Pigs'. Christine, a seamstress for pop bands, supported the family for some years but is unable to compete with the industrialization of her trade, and is irked by Rex's melancholy, failure to provide, and their debt-ridden existence. After frequent rows they separate.

Angry, hurt and disorientated by his father's departure, Gabriel escapes into his imaginary 'glass-walled world' that he sees in the mirror, which is always more palatable than reality,

and where he plays out his fantasises of becoming a film director
(*G* 17). The novel is centrally concerned with the power of the
imagination. At one level, the title refers to Gabriel's talent as an
artist and photographer. The novel explores the nature of the
creative process, the passion it inspires and the difficulty of
nurturing it. Gabriel's gift is also the picture that rock star Lester
Jones (Rex's old friend in whose band he once played) gives him.
Lester's continued fame makes the painting a valuable item. The
plot is structured around the clashes that ensue when the family
members differ on what should be done with the picture.
Characteristically, Rex sees it as a short-term solution to his
money problems, for Christine it is an investment and Gabriel
insists it is his. Gabriel draws two copies and gives one to each
parent, keeping the original. Kureishi uses the conflicts over the
picture to explore the emotional terrain of relationships
between parents, and with their children. Despite a creaky plot
structure, with rather strained efforts to weave events around
the painting (and the chance visit to Lester), this device is
employed much more effectively than the search for a pair of
shoes that performed a similar cohesive function in *London Kills
Me*. In contrast to the screenplay, Kureishi creates an absorbing
social world in his dramatization of the tensions and conflicting
expectations in family relationships, making the novel both
concrete and universal.

Kureishi successfully narrates the story through a youth's
perspective. On the whole, Kureishi unobtrusively braids a
turbulent adolescent boy's view with a more mature vision and
acute observations of humanity, although occasionally Gabriel's
perceptions seem to be those of an older man inserted into the
mouth of a younger boy with a jarring effect. At the same time,
Gabriel's maturity beyond his years is plausible, accelerated by
his parents' unstable relationship. Characteristically Kureishi
provides a fresh take on the subject of parenting with a reversal
of roles. It is Gabriel who is protective of his mother and
instrumental in encouraging his father and securing him a
steady job as a music teacher. As a 'divorce go-between', Gabriel
shields one parent from the other and secures their reunion by
adopting the matchmaker's role. Gabriel's fierce, possessive love
of his mother is moving and convincing. Christine is Kureishi's
most sympathetic mother figure: passionate, vulnerable, jug-

gling her family's demands and her own desires. However, it is the father–son relationship, characterized by intense affection and rivalry, that takes centre stage. Kureishi's oblique approach enables him to glean fresh insights on the raising of children and familial relationships from this conventionally 'disfunctional' family. Rex is both feckless and irresponsible and his yearning for an 'alternative' lifestyle and recourse to the past is sent up. However, the novel sympathetically portrays his opposition to formal education and his sense of the importance of letting children learn and experience life for themselves, but only when they are old enough. This is illustrated in the incident where he strays from his usual liberal position, forbidding Gabriel to hang out with older youth squatting in the 'drum', a flat full of stolen goods and drugs (G 17).

The novel's cheerful tone is evidenced in the way Kureishi shares a joke with his readers with the reference to Deedee Osgood from *The Black Album*, now a therapist. Karim Amir and Charlie Hero make a cameo appearance, still competing with each other and as 'frivolous and self-absorbed' as ever (G 123), although this lighter vein is tinged with more sober reflections: we learn Haroon and Eva are dead. This is not the unalloyed hilarity and ebullience of *Buddha*; the humour in *Gabriel's Gift* is bitter-sweet. This poignancy stems in part from the confusions and unhappiness caused by the breakdown of Christine and Rex's relationship, and from the insights we are given into all the characters' vulnerability. In previous novels we are not encouraged to empathize with the characters to this degree. The death of Gabriel's identical twin brother Archie (at the age of 2) also casts a shadow over the novel. Its shattering impact is delineated sensitively, contrasting Gabriel and his father's continued communication with Archie with Christine's different strategy of coping in her insistence, with clenched palms, that Archie is never coming back. The novel is permeated with images of reflection. In Gabriel's mirror he sees his remembered twin, who is both his mirror image and invisible mentor in a parallel existence. Archie represents endless possibilities of what might have been and offers Gabriel an alternative perspective; when in doubt Gabriel looks at the world through Archie's eyes.

In many ways the characters are too alive for the rather heavy-handed plot. The happy ending feels contrived, with

119

Christine conveniently 'chucked' by her new boyfriend Albert the day before Rex asks her to accompany him to a dinner, for moral support, which paves the way to their reunion. The North London setting is updated and increasingly international. Its multicultural mix now includes every race, including the caricatured au pair Hannah, a refugee from a former communist country. The novel is not as self-consciously date-stamped as *Black Album*, although there are fleeting references to Tracey Emin's canvas tent and Damien Hirst's creations.

Gabriel's Gift marks a new direction for Kureishi. Its characters at first seem derailed, but are no longer terminally dislocated or disconnected. Kureishi seems to be over his immersion in misery and emptiness. This novella differs from his earlier novels, with both gains and losses. *Gabriel's Gift* does not juggle several subplots in the manner of *Buddha*, so this shorter novel is more streamlined, allowing Kureishi to probe deeper. At the same time, without the wide range of characters (some rich, others shadowy) whose disparate lives intersect, the rumbustious, chaotic and fast-paced quality is missing.

The resonances between his early and more recent work underscore Kureishi's consistent preoccupation with the conflicting claims of individualism and communal values, pointing to his sustained interest in a spectrum of relationships between an individual and his or her family, lover, 'ethnic' or religious community and nation. Refracted through the perspectives of parents, children and lovers, Kureishi's work explores how one defines oneself within these groups and attempts to reconcile competing demands.

Afterword

Kureishi shot to fame with his self-conscious counters to mainstream formulations. Today he is fêted by Channel 4, the Arts Council of England who funded *My Son the Fanatic* and the British Council. While this is a measure of the success of Kureishi among others in penetrating mainstream media institutions and their contribution towards demarginalizing minority artistic production in Britain, equally it is an indication of the extent to which Kureishi's politics, particularly his celebration of liberal multiculturalism, occupies the centre-ground.

Kureishi emerged in the 1980s, 'a decade consumed by identity politics and claims to authenticity through marginalised subjectivities'.[1] However, then as now he is not concerned to incite white liberal guilt and sympathy over the hierarchies of oppression that minorities occupy. Instead, his work subverts and transgresses dominant notions of national and ethnic, gendered and sexual identity, and asks probing questions about all forms of authority, affiliations and ideologies. This move is embodied in the way Kureishi's texts draw on a Brechtian aesthetic performing conflicts and putting the onus on the viewer or reader to take a position, forcing them to think and see the familiar afresh. He achieves this with his use of realism undercut by satire, elements of farce and comic exaggeration and pervasive ironic distance. His early screenplays and narratives are often focalized around a particular character, allowing a glimpse of interiority, only to withdraw, distancing the reader/viewer by mocking the character and never allowing over-identification. In his later fiction the reader is relentlessly wedged inside the character, but again to an alienating effect.

In terms of cultural representation, Britain today is very different from the 1980s when Kureishi first came to the fore.

Over the last ten years British Asian cultural forms have penetrated mainstream popular culture in terms of fashion, cinema and TV and pop music of Cornershop and Talvin Singh. Kureishi played and continues to play an important role in this. Kureishi's *My Beautiful Laundrette* and *Sammy and Rosie Get Laid* helped create an identifiably British Asian cinema. They gave several British-born Asian actors and actresses much publicity. These younger artists in turn are involved in the media, creating roles for other British Asians, expanding definitions of minority identities in their own writing and pointing to the many differences between those that share the designation of Asian origin. Rita Wolf (who played Tania in *Laundrette*) co-founded the Kali Theatre group with writer Rukhsana Ahmad. Gordon Warneke (who played Omar in *Laundrette*) acted subsequently in *Blood*. Ayub Khan Din (who played Sammy in *Sammy and Rosie*) went on to write the play and screenplay of *East is East* (which won the *Evening Standard*'s best British film award in 1999). *Sammy and Rosie* provided Meera Syal (writer of *Bhaji on the Beach*, 1994, co-writer and performer of the hit British Asian TV comedy *Goodness Gracious Me*) with her first film role.

However, Kureishi's most important influence lies in his trademark political irreverence towards his subjects. Meera Syal observes: 'although Kureishi was not a conscious influence on my work, his ability to satirize the sacred cows was obviously part of my growing up here. He was also very hip, the first hip Asian in the arts as far as I can recall.'[2] His talent and confidence inspire younger British Asians. Sukhdev Sandhu suggests 'Kureishi's language was a revelation. It was neither meek nor subservient'. His 'playful and casually knowing voice' made him a 'talismanic figure' for young Asians.[3] Kureishi's legacy is equally his refusal to be pigeonholed as an 'ethnic' writer. While Kureishi is most highly acclaimed for his tales of race and sexuality, *Laundrette* and *Buddha*, his cross-over appeal, stemming from his humour, pleasurable prose, and shrewd insights into contemporary mores and modern urban experiences, make him one of the foremost writers of his generation.

Notes

INTRODUCTION: SITUATING HANIF KUREISHI

1. See also Salman Rushdie, 'The New Empire in Britain' (1982), reprinted in Salman Rushdie, *Imaginary Homelands* (London: Granta, 1991), 129–38.
2. Significantly, in the *Times Literary Supplement*'s review of 'The Rainbow Sign' published with the script of *My Beautiul Laundrette*, Ian Jack supports the 'quieter humanist voice' of the screenplay rather than Kureishi's suggestion in the essay that the white British must make the 'adjustments'. The reviewer argues the 'poor British whites already feel put-upon and have made more "adjustments" to the bewildering changes in their economic and social life over the past twenty years than any other social class in Western Europe'. See Ian Jack, 'Brutish Way of Life: *My Beautiful Laundrette*, and *The Rainbow Sign* (book review)', *Times Literary Supplement*, 2 May 1986, 470.
3. The discursive construct of 'race' operates biologically, however much it may be defined as, or substituted with, 'ethnicity' today. Race is deployed in this book in terms of the oppressive effects of this discursive formation. Ethnicity refers to the politically and culturally constructed nature of identity, rather than an originary essence.
4. Paul Gilroy, 'Cultural Studies and Ethnic Absolutism', in Lawrence Grossberg and Cary Nelson and Paula Treichler (eds.), *Cultural Studies* (London: Routledge, 1990), 188.
5. Kureishi began to write at the age of 14 as a way of coping with and communicating his experiences of racism. Interviews convey his isolation: 'it was like writing about racism was like writing messages in a bottle. This has happened to me, has it happened to you?' See Ginny Douglas, 'Sex and Spying in Suburbia', *Observer*, 1 April 1990, 65.

6. Ania Loomba, *Colonialism/Postcolonialism* (London: Routledge, 1998), 122.
7. Black and black British are shifting and contested terms. Stuart Hall describes how 'black' was coined in the seventies and eighties as a political category and as a strategic, collective definition to describe all ethnic minorities who were subject to oppression. See Stuart Hall, 'New Ethnicities', in Kobena Mercer (ed.), *Black Film, British Cinema* (London: Institute of Contemporary Arts, 1988), 27. I use the term black in this way to indicate inclusively African-Caribbean and Asian communities. For specific reference, African-Caribbean or Asian is used. By contrast, Tariq Modood questions the black anti-racist model, arguing that there is no common positive identity behind the idea of 'black' and that Asians are subsumed in such a labelling, because many people use the term 'black' to refer to African-Caribbean communities exclusively. Tariq Modood, *Not Easy Being British: Colour, Culture and Citizenship* (London: Trentham Books Limited, 1992), 20.
8. See also A. Robert Lee, 'Changing the Script: Sex, Lies and Videotapes in Hanif Kureishi, David Dabydeen and Mike Philips', in A. Robert Lee (ed.), *Other Britain, Other British: Contemporary Multicultural Fiction* (London: Pluto Press, 1995), 69–89.
9. Elyse Singer, 'Hanif Kureishi: A Londoner, But Not a Brit', in Melissa Biggs (ed.), *In the Vernacular: Interviews at Yale with the Sculptors of Culture* (Jefferson, NC: McFarland and Col., 1991), 108.
10. This is not necessarily the case for those from Scotland, Ireland and Wales.
11. Anuradha Dingwaney Needham, *Using the Master's Tools: Resistance and the Literature of the African and South Asian Diasporas* (Houndmills: Macmillan, 2000), 154, n. 5.
12. Simon Gikandi, *Maps of Englishness* (New York: Columbia University Press, 1996), 204.
13. Black British writing refers to the literatures written in English by people who originate from the former colonies of Africa, the Caribbean and Asia.
14. Peter Childs, *Post-colonial Theory and English Literature* (Edinburgh: Edinburgh University Press, 1999), 25, 23.
15. Hanif Kureishi, Cheltenham Literary Festival, 17 October 1997.
16. Kureishi emphasizes this point in interviews. See 'In the Chair' with Professor Anthony Clare on Radio 4, 9 October 1998.
17. The recent independent report launched by the government on *The Future of Multi-ethnic Britain* argues that Britain needs to re-imagine itself as a genuinely multicultural country. This is precisely the challenge that Kureishi posed fifteen years ago in 'The Rainbow Sign'. As Gary Younge comments, the hostile reactions to the

124

report's section on the 'racial connotations' of the term 'British' (interpreted by right-wing commentators as an affront to the 'native' British and as an attempt to rewrite – what is significantly referred to as 'our' history) are a gauge of 'the racial temperature in Britain'. Younge suggests the responses indicate that 'we are no closer to having a mature and open debate on race in this country'. See Gary Younge, 'The Runnymede Report', *Guardian*, 11 October 2000, 7.

18. Frank Kermode, 'Voice of the Almost English', *Guardian*, 10 April 1990, 42.
19. J. B. Miller, 'For His Film, Hanif Kureishi reaches for a "Beautiful Laundrette"', *New York Times*, 2 August 1992, 16.
20. See Edward Said, 'Reflections on Exile', *Granta*, 13 (1984), 172 and Rushdie, *Imaginary Homelands*, 19.
21. The relationship between Kureishi's work and Bhabha's theorizing of hybridity will be examined in chapter 4.
22. Salman Rushdie, *Imaginary Homelands*, 17.
23. Reviews of Kureishi's adaptation of Brecht's *Mother Courage and Her Children* emphasize the colloquial, explicit nature of Kureishi's script. See Lloyd Rose, 'A Great Display of "Courage"', *Washington Post*, 13 April 1993, section B, 1. See also Cynthia Carey's analysis of Kureishi's language in Cynthia Carey, 'Hanif Kureishi's *The Buddha of Suburbia* as a Post-Colonial Novel', *Commonwealth Essays and Studies*, SP: 4 (1997), 119–25.
24. John Haffenden, 'An Interview with Salman Rushdie', *Literary Review*, September 1983, 31.
25. Sukhdev Sandhu, 'Pop Goes the Centre: Hanif Kureishi's London', in Laura Chrisman and Benita Parry (eds.), *Postcolonial Theory and Criticism* (Cambridge: D. S. Brewer, 2000), 152.
26. Colin MacCabe, 'Interview: Hanif Kureishi on London', *Critical Quarterly*, 41/3 (1999), 37.
27. See also Sandhu, 'Pop Goes the Centre', in Chrisman and Parry (eds.), *Postcolonial Theory* for an insightful, detailed exploration of the significance of London in Kureishi's work.
28. Singer, 'Hanif Kureishi: A Londoner, But not a Brit', in Biggs (ed.), *In the Vernacular*, 105. The English Stage Company based at the Royal Court Theatre was founded in 1956 by George Devine to present modern plays and encourage new dramatists. Since its inception it has been characterized by its anti-establishment, progressive ethos, presenting important new work by John Osborne, Samuel Beckett, Edward Bond, Joe Orton, Caryl Churchill, and the influential Caribbean playwright Mustapha Mutura.
29. Kenneth C. Kaleta, *Hanif Kureishi* (Austin, TX: University of Texas Press, 1998), 27–8.

30. Alamgir Hasmir, 'Hanif Kureishi and the Tradition of the Novel', *The International Fiction Review*, 19/2 (1993), 90–92.
31. Paul Gilroy, *The Black Atlantic* (London: Verso, 1993), ix, 16.
32. Ann Treneman, 'Revelations: I Thought, I'll be a Writer', *Independent*, 15 April, 1997, 10.
33. Homi Bhabha unpacks the traditional notion of cultural translation where the translator bridges separate cultures. For Bhabha, culture is 'untranslatable' in this traditional sense because it is always already mixed with other cultures. The mixing of cultures and languages in migrant and border cultures occurs constantly. See Bhabha, 'How Newness enters the World: Postmodern Space, Postcolonial Times and the Trials of Cultural Translation', in *The Location of Culture* (London: Routledge, 1994). Recent translation studies emphasize the precarious, ambivalent and mediated nature of cultural translation. See Rey Chow, *Primitive Passions: Visuality, Sexuality, Ethnography* and *Contemporary Chinese Cinema* (New York: Columbia University Press, 1995).
34. As Trinh T. Minh-ha observes, there is a range of positions on the 'outsider–insider' spectrum. See Trinh T. Minh-ha, *Cinema Interval* (London: Routledge, 1999), 58.
35. Abdul JanMohamed, 'Wordliness-Without-World, Homelessness-as-Home: Towards a Definition of the Specular Border Intellectual', in Michael Sprinker (ed.), *Edward Said: A Critical Reader* (Cambridge: MA: Blackwell, 1992), 105.
36. JanMohamed, 'Worldliness-Without-World', in Sprinker (ed.), *Edward Said*, 103.
37. Coco Fusco, 'Fantasies of Oppositionality – Reflections on Recent Conferences in Boston and New York', *Screen*, 29/4 (1988), 91.
38. Ali Rattansi, 'Changing the Subject? Racism, Culture and Education', in James Donald and Ali Rattansi (eds.), *Race, Culture and Difference* (London: Sage Publications in association with The Open University, 1992), 34.
39. Philip Dodd, 'Requiem for a Rave', *Sight and Sound*, 5/1 (1991), 11.
40. MacCabe, 'Interview: Hanif Kureishi on London', 46.
41. Alison Donnell, 'Editorial – Dressing with a Difference: Cultural Representation, Minority Rights and Ethnic Chic', *Interventions*, 1/4 (1999), 496.
42. Miller, 'For His Film, Hanif Kureishi reaches for a "Beautiful Laundrette"', 16.
43. Kureishi, preface to the screenplay of *Intimacy*, forthcoming.
44. The exception to this trajectory is Kureishi's *London Kills Me*, released in 1991, which is not concerned with issues of ethnicity or race.
45. In this context, 'separatist activism', refers to vigilante resistance to white racism.

CHAPTER 1. KUREISHI'S DISCOVERY OF HIS SUBJECT IN HIS EARLY PLAYS

1. The 1981 British Nationality Act removed the automatic right of all children born in the UK to be citizens. Subsequently, in 1987, the Carriers' Liability Act cut the number seeking asylum by half. In the same year, visa requirements were introduced for visitors from five Asian and African countries. Most controversial was the new bill introduced to restrict family reunion.
2. Hanif Kureishi, *Playscript 102* (London: John Calder, 1983).
3. Irving Wardle, '*The King and Me*' (review), *The Times*, 9 January 1980, 11.
4. Irving Wardle, 'Collision of Cultures: *The Mother Country*' (review), *The Times*, 23 July 1980, 13.
5. James Fenton, '"Okay as a Favour, Tell You What I'll Do"', *Sunday Times*, 25 September 1983, 39.
6. Michael Billington, '*Outskirts*' (review), *Guardian*, 29 April 1981, 10.
7. Irving Wardle, 'A Moral Tale that Carries Conviction', *The Times*, 29 April 1981, 12.
8. Dick Hebdige, *Subculture: The Meaning of Style* (London: Methuen, 1979), 73.
9. Avtar Brah, *Cartographies of Diaspora: Contesting Identities* (London: Routledge, 1996), 43. For an account of the first-generation struggles, see A. Sivanandan, *From Resistance to Rebellion: Asian and Afro-Caribbean Struggles in Britain* (London: Institute of Race Relations), 1986.
10. Brah, *Cartographies of Diaspora*, 47, 44.
11. Gordon Brook Shepherd, 'Where the Blame for Brixton Lies', *Sunday Telegraph*, 19 April 1981, 16.
12. Cited in David Noakes, 'Anthem for Doomed Youth?', *Times Literary Supplement*, 4 December 1981, 1427.
13. As Alan Fountain suggests, Channel 4's refusal to transmit Ceddo's *The People's Account* stemmed from 'seeing teenage people saying, "this isn't going to work any more, we are going to destabilise society until you take an interest in what we have got to say"'. See Alan Fountain, 'Channel 4 and Black Independents', in Kobena Mercer (ed.), *Black Film British Cinema* (London: ICA, 1988), 43. Perhaps, in contrast, Kureishi's work was more amenable to the British arts establishment because it was less confrontational. *Borderline* was never staged in Southall as originally conceived because of objections by local British Asians. These may have originated from a perception that the play was oriented towards a white audience.

14. Kureishi observes: 'The real problem when I was growing up was that racism just wasn't a topic of understanding in England...there was no wider understanding of racism. You felt it was your own personal and psychological problem'. Cited in Glenn Collins, 'Screen Writer Turns to the Novel to Tell of Race and Class in London', *New York Times*, 24 May 1990, 17.
15. David Theo Goldberg, *Multiculturalism: A Critical Reader* (Oxford: Blackwell, 1994), 12.
16. Irving Wardle *'Borderline'* (review), *The Times*, 6 November 1981, 18.
17. James Fenton, '"What Did You Sell in the War, Daddy?"', *Sunday Times*, 8 November 1981, 41.
18. Noakes, 'Anthem for Doomed Youth?', 1427.
19. Gayatri Chakravorty Spivak, *Outside in the Teaching Machine* (London: Routledge 1993), 250.
20. Irving Wardle, '"Us and Them...and Those": *Birds of Passage* (review), *The Times*, 17 September 1983, 9 (emphasis mine).

CHAPTER 2: THE POLITICS OF REPRESENTATION: POLITICAL COMMITMENT AND IRONIC DISTANCE

1. Cited in Sheila Johnston, 'Plain Dealing', *Independent*, 7 March 1991, 15.
2. Salman Rushdie, *Imaginary Homelands* (London: Granta, 1991), 92.
3. Elyse Singer, 'Hanif Kureishi: A Londoner, But Not a Brit', in Melissa Biggs (ed.), *In the Vernacular: Interviews at Yale with the Sculptors of Culture* (Jefferson, NC: McFarland and Co., 1991), 109.
4. Thatcher lowered tax to encourage business and valorized an ethos of individualism.
5. For example, in contrast to Mahmood Jamal's *Majdar* (Retake Film and Video Collective, 1984).
6. Kobena Mercer, *Welcome to the Jungle: New Positions in Black Cultural Studies* (London: Routledge, 1994), 214.
7. Pratibha Parma, 'Sammy and Rosie Get Laid', *Marxism Today*, 32 (1988), 39.
8. Stuart Hall, 'New Ethnicities', in Kobena Mercer (ed.), *Black Film, British Cinema* (London: Institute of Contemporary Arts, 1988), 28.
9. Hall, 'New Ethnicities', in Mercer (ed.), *Black Film, British Cinema*, 29. For an insightful account of the implications of Kureishi/Frears's subversion of heterosexism and racism, see Radhika Mohanram, 'Postcolonial Spaces and Deterritorialised (Homo)Sexuality: The Films of Hanif Kureishi', in Gita Rajan and Radhika Mohanram (eds.), *Postcolonial Discourse and Changing Cultural Contexts: Theory*

and Criticism (Westport, CT: Greenwood Press, 1995), 117–34.

10. Hall, 'New Ethnicities', in Mercer (ed.), *Black Film, British Cinema*, 27.

11. Jane Root, 'Scenes from a Marriage', *Monthly Film Bulletin*, 52/622 (1985), 333.

12. Julian Henriques, 'Realism and the New Language', in Mercer (ed.), *Black Film, British Cinema*, 19.

13. Hanif Kureishi, 'One Year On', *Guardian*, 21 February 2000, 15.

14. Gayatri Chakravorty Spivak, *Outside in the Teaching Machine* (London: Routledge 1993), 249.

15. Ian Jack, 'Brutish Way of Life: *My Beautiful Laundrette*, and *The Rainbow Sign*' (book review), *Times Literary Supplement*, 2 May 1986, 470.

16. Perminder Dhillon-Kashyap, 'Locating the Asian Experience', *Screen*, 29/4 (1988), 125.

17. Robert Stam and Ella Shohat, *Unthinking Eurocentrism* (London: Routledge, 1994), 181.

18. Hanif Kureishi, 'Disposing of the Raj', *Marxism Today*, January 1987, 43.

19. Mahmood Jamal, 'Dirty Linen', in Mercer (ed.), *Black Film, British Cinema*, 21. Ironically, some black critics and right-wing white critics coincide in their hostility to what they see as the universalistic implications of different aspects of Kureishi's representations. Jamal critiques *Laundrette*'s portrayal of London's Pakistani community. In Norman Stone's review of both films, he argues, 'there are nasty patches in modern Britain, and parts of our great cities are a disgrace. ... But the vision of England they provide ... represent a tiny part of modern England.' See Norman Stone, 'Through a Lens Darkly: Sick Scenes from English Life', *Sunday Times,* 10 January 1988, reprinted in Mercer (ed.), *Black Film, British Cinema*, 22–4.

20. Kobena Mercer, 'Diaspora Culture and the Dialogic Imagination: The Aesthetics of Black Independent Film in Britain', in Mbye B. Cham and Claire Andrade-Watkins (eds.), *Black Frames: Critical Perspectives on Black Independent Cinema* (Cambridge, MA: MIT Press, 1988), 53.

21. Shohat and Stam, *Unthinking Eurocentrism*, 215, 214.

22. Inderpal Grewal, 'Salman Rushdie: Marginality, Women and *Shame*', in M. D. Fletcher (ed.), *Reading Rushdie: Perspectives on the Fiction of Salman Rushdie* (Amsterdam: Rodopi, 1994), 132, n. 12 (emphasis mine).

23. Contrast Meera Syal's portrayals of British Asian women who attempt to redefine what being an Asian/woman means from within the community, 'always proud to be who they were, but not scared to push back the boundaries'. See Meera Syal, *Life Isn't All Ha Ha Hee Hee* (London: Doubleday 1999), 84.

24. For an opposing point of view, see Elisabeth de Cacqueray, 'Constructions of Women in British Cinema: From Losey/Pinter's Modernism to the Postmodernism of Frears/Kureishi', in *Caliban*, 32 (1995), 109–20.
25. Cited in Perminder Dhillon-Kashyap, 'Locating the Asian Experience', *Screen*, 29/4 (1988), 125.
26. Rita Wolf, 'Beyond the Laundrette', *Guardian*, 14 February 1987, 14.
27. Jane Root, 'Scenes from a Marriage', *Monthly Film Bulletin*, 52/622 (1985), 333.
28. Hanif Kureishi, Cheltenham Literary Festival, 17 October 1997.
29. Kenneth C. Kaleta, *Hanif Kureishi* (Austin, TX: University of Texas Press, 1998), 220 (emphasis mine).
30. Homi Bhabha identifies the anxieties underlying the proliferation of stereotypes: 'The stereotype is a complex, ambivalent, contradictory mode of representation, as anxious as it is assertive'. Stereotypes cannot be proved, so 'must be told (compulsively) again and afresh'. See Homi Bhabha, *The Location of Culture* (London: Routledge, 1994), 70, 77.
31. Jamal, 'Dirty Linen', in Mercer (ed.), *Black Film, British Cinema*, 21.
32. Cited in Kobena Mercer 'Recoding Narratives of Race and Nation', in Mercer (ed.), *Black Film, British Cinema* 12.
33. Lester Friedman and Scott Stewart, 'Keeping His Own Voice: An Interview with Stephen Frears', in Wheeler Winston Dixon, *Re-Viewing British Cinema, 1900–1992: Essays and Interviews* (Albany: State University of New York Press, 1994), 233.
34. Glenn Collins, 'Screen Writer Turns to the Novel to Tell of Race and Class in London', *New York Times*, 24 May 1990, 17 (emphasis mine).
35. J. B. Miller, 'For His Film, Hanif Kureishi Reaches for a 'Beautiful Laundrette', *New York Times*, 2 August 1992, 16.
36. Perhaps Tariq Mehmood's more overt politically activist tones were less palatable than Kureishi's liberal multiculturalism.
37. Isaac Julien and Kobena Mercer, 'De Margin and De Centre', *Screen*, 29/4 (1988), 4.
38. Friedman and Stewart, 'Keeping His Own Voice', in Dixon *Re-Viewing British Cinema*, 233.
39. Sneja Gnew and Gayatri Chakravorty Spivak, 'Questions of Multiculturalism', in Mary Broe and Angela Ingram (eds.), *Women's Writing in Exile* (Chapel Hill: University of North Carolina Press, 1989), 414.
40. Uma Narayan, *Dislocating Cultures. Identities, Traditions, and Third-World Feminism* (London: Routledge, 1997), 142.
41. Jamal, 'Dirty Linen', in Mercer (ed.), *Black Film, British Cinema*, 21.
42. Hall, *New Ethnicities*, in Mercer (ed.), *Black Film, British Cinema*, 30. See also Spivak, *Outside in the Teaching Machine*, 253.

43. Rushdie, 'Minority Literatures in a Multi-cultural Society', in Kirsten Holste Peterson and Anna Rutherford (eds.), *Displaced Persons* (Sydney: Dangaroo Press, 1992), 41.
44. Rushdie, 'Minority Literatures', in Holste Peterson and Rutherford, (eds.), *Displaced Persons*, 41.
45. Colin MacCabe, 'Interview: Hanif Kureishi on London', *Critical Quarterly*, 41/3 (1999), 38, 41.
46. Hanif Kureishi, 'Dirty Washing', *Time Out*, 795 (14–20 November 1985), 25–6.
47. Friedman and Stewart, 'Keeping His Own Voice' in Dixon, *Re-Viewing British Cinema*, 228.
48. Mercer, *Welcome to the Jungle*, 259.
49. bell hooks entitles her essay on Kureishi, 'Stylish Nihilism: Race, Sex and Class at the Movies'. See bell hooks, *Yearning: Race, Gender and Class Politics* (Boston: South End Press, 1991), 155.
50. 'Ceddo: The People's Account', in Mercer (ed.), *Black Film British Cinema*, 58.
51. Spivak, *Outside in the Teaching Machine*, 244.
52. As Nahem Yousaf suggests, Danny's characterization contests the state's criminalization of black communities. See 'Hanif Kureishi and "the Brown Man's Burden"', *Critical Survey*, 8/1 (1996), 20.
53. bell hooks, *Yearning*, 160.
54. Ibid.
55. This heterosexism culminated in the introduction of Section 28 of the 1988 Local Government Act which forbade local authorities from promoting homosexuality or depicting homosexuals in a 'pretended family relationship'. Kureishi amongst others vehemently opposed this law.
56. In March 1982 Thatcher observes: 'We are reaping what was sown in the sixties.. fashionable theories and permissive clap-trap set the scene for a society in which the old virtues of discipline and restraint were denigrated', cited in Arthur Marwick, *British Society Since 1945* (London: Penguin, 1990), 10. Right-wing groups mobilized in opposition to the permisssive legislation of the 1960s, which reformed laws on homosexuality, abortion, censorship and divorce.
57. Cited in Kaleta, *Hanif Kureishi*, 56.
58. Friedman and Stewart, 'Keeping His Own Voice', in Dixon, *Re-Viewing British Cinema*, 233.
59. Leonard Quart, '*Sammy and Rosie Get Laid*' (review), *Cineaste* (1988), 41.
60. This is a less acknowledged but implicit part of the burden of representation.
61. hooks, *Yearning*, 159.

62. Ibid., 161.
63. Ibid., 159
64. Kureishi, 'Disposing of the Raj', *Marxism Today*, January 1987, 43.
65. hooks, *Yearning*, 163.
66. Cited in David Nicholson, 'My Beautiful Britain', *Films and Filming*, January 1988, 10.

CHAPTER 3: CULTURE AND IDENTITY

1. Colin MacCabe, 'Interview: Hanif Kureishi on London', *Critical Quarterly*, 41/3 (1999), 42. Clark Blaise reads the novel's episodic plotting, competing subplots and quick cuts as evidence of the screenwriter's failure to adapt to the novel form. See Clark Blaise, 'A Guru by Night', *New York Times*, 6 May 1990, 20. Conversely Kureishi constructs *Buddha* in a visual, filmic mode, enriching the novel form with cinematic action in, for example, the dramatic opening, where we witness Haroon's yoga antics, and in the episode where Karim as a voyeur observes his father having sex with Eva.
2. Glenn Collins, 'Screen Writer Turns to the Novel to Tell of Race and Class in London', *New York Times*, 24 May 1990, 17.
3. For a detailed account of Kureishi's appropriation of the *Bildungsroman*, see Judith Misrahi-Barak, 'Yoga and the *Bildungsroman* in Hanif Kureishi's *The Buddha of Suburbia*', *Commonwealth Essays and Studies*, SP: 4 (1997), 88–94.
4. These aspects were heightened in the BBC's close adaptation of the novel in 1993, which Kureishi describes as a 'costume drama', with an evocative score composed by David Bowie. Kureishi describes the process of adapting his first-person novel into a screenplay in his essay 'The Boy in the Bedroom'. See also Colin MacCabe, 'Interview: Hanif Kureishi on London', *Critical Quarterly*, 41/3 (1999), 43.
5. Nahem Yousaf, 'Hanif Kureishi and "the Brown Man's Burden"', *Critical Survey*, 8/1 (1996), 18.
6. British Asians' divergent responses to the BBC TV adaptation of *The Buddha of Suburbia* suggest that the internal debates on the politics of representation within the British Asian community (particularly over the explicit sexual scenes between Karim and Jamila) remain as heated as ever. An article in the *Daily Telegraph* cites Kali Ruddi, a Hindu town councillor's observations: 'That series has done untold damage to the British perceptions of Asians in this country. The older generation are shown to be old-fashioned and the younger generation outrageously rebellious and offensively promiscuous.

There is no middle ground. What is worse, people are applying these caricatures to Asians in the 90's. Things are not so extreme.' The article goes on to cite young Asian women brought up in Britain who disagreed with Ruddi's verdict. These young women suggest that their strict upbringing encouraged them to experiment sexually in ways similar to those depicted in *The Buddha of Suburbia*. One woman, Sita, is quoted as saying 'the only shocking thing was the degree of explicitness on TV But it was all going on among many of us, even more so today.' Another Asian woman suggests that 'us women have tended to westernise a lot more than the men because it is in our interests. I think the men have got left behind.' This points to the gendered nature of the differing responses to Kureishi's representations. At the same time, the emphasis of the *Daily Telegraph* article conforms to standard Eurocentric assumptions of freeing brown women from brown men. See Tessa Boase, 'Embarrassed by the Buddha', *Daily Telegraph*, 25 November 1993, 16.

7. Kenneth C. Kaleta, *Hanif Kureishi* (Austin, TX: University of Texas Press, 1998), 220.

8. Kureishi comments: 'I think it would be dangerous for writers to have too much of a sense of responsibility'. See Colin MacCabe, 'Interview: Hanif Kureishi on London', *Critical Quarterly*, 41/3 (1999), 53.

9. Gayatri Chakravorty Spivak, 'The Burden of English Studies', in Rajeswari Sunder Rajan (ed.), *The Lie of the Land: English Literary Studies in India* (Delhi: Oxford University Press, 1992), 293, n. 26.

10. Paul Gilroy, *The Black Atlantic* (London: Verso), 1993, 2.

11. Gilroy, *The Black Atlantic*, 2.

12. Cited in Donald Weber, ' "No Secrets Were Safe from Me": Situating Hanif Kureishi', *The Massachusetts Review*, 38/1 (1997), 125.

13. Paul Gilroy, *There ain't no Black in the Union Jack: Cultural Politics of Race and Nation* (London: Hutchinson, 1987), 13.

14. 'The performative is not a singular act used by an already established subject, but one of the powerful and insidious ways in which subjects are called into being from diffuse social quarters, inaugurated into sociality by a variety of powerful and diffuse interpellations.' See Judith Butler, *Gender Trouble* (London: Routledge, 1990), 160. See also Sara Salih, *Judith Butler* (London: Routledge, forthcoming).

15. Philip Dodd, 'Requiem for a Rave', *Sight and Sound*, 5/1 (1991), 10.

16. Ibid.

17. Jamila's contempt for Karim echoes Zeeny's mockery of Saladin in Rushdie's *The Satanic Verses*. Zeeny teases Saladin as one 'who has to travel to wog-land with some two-bit company playing the babu

part on top of it, just to get into a play'. See Salman Rushdie, *The Satanic Verses* (London: Viking, 1989), 61.

18. See also Nahem Yousaf, 'Hanif Kureishi and "the Brown Man's Burden"', *Critical Survey*, 8/1 (1996), 17.
19. Spivak, 'The Burden of English Studies', in Rajeswari Sunder Rajan (ed.), *The Lie of the Land*, 293.
20. Anuradha Dingwaney Needham, *Using the Master's Tools: Resistance and the Literature of the African and South Asian Diasporas* (Houndmills: Macmillan, 2000), 124.
21. For such a polarization, see Bill Ashcroft, Gareth Griffiths and Helen Tiffin, *The Empire Writes Back* (London: Routledge, 1989), 3–4.
22. Paul Gilroy *The Black Atlantic*, 32.
23. The racializing of gender becomes manifest in Helen's father's attempt to control her sexuality and protect her from the perceived threat posed to her by Karim. Similarly, Karim is 'ecstatic about [his] triumph in seducing' Helen who is now denied individuality and becomes simply 'the dog owner's daughter' (*BS* 82). The way women and their bodies function both biologically and symbolically as the boundaries of the ethnic groups and/or the nation is further underlined in Karim's attempts to defy exclusion by 'possessing' white British women: 'And we pursued English roses as we pursued England; by possessing these prizes, this kindness and beauty, we stared defiantly into the eye of the Empire and all its self-regard' (*BS* 227). See Nira Yuval-Davis and Floya Anthias (eds.), *Woman-Nation-State* (London: Macmillan, 1989).
24. These debates recur in Kureishi's subsequent novel, *The Black Album*, where Chad mocks Shahid's retreat into literature: 'Out there … it's genocide. Rape. Oppression. Murder. The history of the world is – slaughter. And you reading stories like some old grandma' (*BA* 21). This debate becomes part of the novel's contrast between the subversive powers of the imagination and Islamic 'intolerance' of dissent and is heavily weighted against Chad.
25. Sangeeta Ray, 'The Nation in Performance: Bhabha, Mukherjee and Kureishi', in Monika Fludernik (ed.), *Hybridity and Postcolonialism* (Tübingen: Stauffenburg Verlag, 1998), 235.
26. Philip Dodd, 'Requiem for a Rave', *Sight and Sound*, 5/1 (1991), 11.
27. Cited in Sheila Johnston, 'Plain Dealing', *Independent*, 7 March 1991, 15.
28. Sukhdev Sandhu, 'Pop Goes the Centre: Hanif Kureishi's London', in Laura Chrisman and Benita Parry (eds.), *Postcolonial Theory and Criticism* (Cambridge: D. S. Brewer, 2000), 146.
29. Matt Wolf, 'Hanif Kureishi Trades Pen for the Director's Lens', *New York Times*, 14 July 1991, Section 2, 12.
30. Adam Mars-Jones, 'Film', *Independent*, 13 December 1991, 18.

31. Philip Dodd, 'Requiem for a Rave', *Sight and Sound*, 5/1 (1991), 11.
32. Kaleta, *Hanif Kureishi*, 103.
33. Geoff Brown, 'Fun with Distant Relations', *The Times*, 12 December 1991, 19.
34. In retrospect Kureishi comments on *London Kills Me*: 'I am aware that I am not a film director', and expresses his preference for collaborative projects. See Colin MacCabe, 'Interview: Hanif Kureishi on London', *Critical Quarterly*, 41/3 (1999), 42.

CHAPTER 4: MUSLIMOPHOBIA

1. Cited in Maya Jaggi, 'A Buddy from Suburbia', *Guardian*, 1 March 1995, 6–7.
2. Tariq Modood, '"Difference", Cultural Racism and Anti-Racism', in Pnina Werbner and Tariq Modood (eds.), *Debating Cultural Hybridity: Multi-Cultural Identities and the Politics of Anti-Racism* (London: Zed Books, 1997), 164.
3. Tariq Modood, 'British Muslims and the Rushdie Affair', in James Donald and Ali Rattansi (eds.), *Race, Culture and Difference* (London: Sage Publications in association with The Open University, 1992), 261. The Labour Force Survey (1992–1999) reports that Pakistani and Bangladeshi communities have the highest unemployment rate and lowest economic activity and employment rate of all Britain's ethnic minorities (Office for National Statistics).
4. Modood, 'British Muslims', in Donald and Rattansi (eds.), *Race*, 268.
5. Modood, '"Difference"', in Werbner and Modood (eds.), *Debating Cultural Hybridity*, 164–5.
6. Commission for Racial Equality, 'Stereotyping and Racism in Britain – an Attitude Survey', in *Impact*, October/November 1999, 41. The Runnymede report observes that aggressive hostility to Islam is expressed in ways unthinkable in relation to other beliefs; see 'The Runnymede Report', *Guardian*, 11 October 2000, 6.
7. Tariq Modood, 'Introduction', in Tariq Modood and Pnina Werbner (eds.), *The Politics of Multiculturalism in the New Europe: Racism, Identity and Community* (London: Zed Books, 1997), 3.
8. In *The Black Album*, Kureishi describes the heightened Islamic fervour amongst the younger generation in Pakistan as a reaction against their parents' 'English accents, foreign degrees and British snobbery' (*BA* 91–2). As this suggests, fundamentalism is also a class issue. Although Kureishi presents the differences between Riaz and Shahid as ideological, they are also classed: the text implicitly contrasts the working-class 'fundamentalist' Muslims with Shahid's anglicized middle-class background.

9. In contrast, David Theo Goldberg proposes an 'incorporation' model of acculturation that envisages a 'dual transformation that takes place in the dominant group and in the insurgent group', although the way this model would be actualized is not straightforward. See David Theo Goldberg, *Multiculturalism: A Critical Reader* (Oxford: Blackwell, 1994), 9.

10. For example, Islam cannot be incorporated within certain models of liberal multiculturalism based on the 'two domains thesis' because in many forms of Islam the division between public and private domains is unacceptable.

11. Political theorists have begun to grapple with these issues. This 'awkward' dilemma is articulated by Charles Taylor:

    all societies are becoming increasingly multicultural, while at the same time becoming more porous. ...more of their members live the life of diaspora, whose center is elsewhere. In these circumstances, there is something awkward about replying simply, 'This is how we do things here.' This reply must be made in cases like the Rushdie controversy, where 'how we do things' covers issues such as the right to life and to freedom of speech. The awkwardness arises from the fact that there are substantial numbers of people who are citizens and also belong to the culture that calls into question our philosophical boundaries. The challenge is to deal with their sense of marginalization without compromising our basic political principles.

    See Charles Taylor 'The Politics of Recognition', in Amy Gutman (ed.), *Multiculturalism: Examining the Politics of Recognition* (Princeton: Princeton University Press, 1994), 63. See also Will Kymlicka, *Multicultural Citizenship: A Liberal Theory of Minority Rights* (Oxford: Clarendon Press, 1996), 154–5. While there has been a development of a significant communitarian strain within liberalism, it is by no means flawless. Modood has critiqued both Kymlicka and Taylor's exclusion of Muslims from their conceptions of multiculturalism, particularly Taylor's implicit assumption (above) that excludes mainstream Muslims from 'the politics of recognition'. See Modood, 'Introduction', in Modood and Werbner (eds.), *The Politics of Multiculturalism in the New Europe*, 3–4. See also Gayatri Chakravorty Spivak's succinct critique of recent works on liberalism and liberal multiculturalism in Gayatri Chakravorty Spivak, *A Critique of Postcolonial Reason: Towards a History of the Vanishing Present* (Cambridge, MA.: Harvard University Press, 1999), 396–7, n. 113.

12. Rushdie's '*The Satanic Verses* ... rejoices in mongrelisation, and fears the absolutism of the Pure'. See Salman Rushdie, *Imaginary Homelands* (London: Granta, 1991), 393–4. In this way both Kureishi and Rushdie define anyone who does not wish to mongrelize his or her traditions as religious extremists. Commentators have noted the exclusivity that informs valorizations of hybridity. Bart Moore-

Gilbert observes, 'doctrines of hybridity do not take sufficient cognizance of those who resist the vision it inscribes. Are all "fundamentalists" or "separatists" to be stripped of their rights in the new dispensation, which some theories of hybridity anticipate?' See Bart Moore-Gilbert, *PostColonial Theory: Contexts, Practices, Politics* (London: Verso, 1997), 195. See also Peter van der Veer 'The Enigma of Arrival: Hybridity and Authenticity in the Global Space', in Werbner and Modood, *Debating Cultural Hybridity*, 102.

13. Ella Shohat, 'Notes on the "Post-colonial"', *Social Text* 31/32 (1993), 110.

14. This disjunction is more pronounced in Rushdie, although see Kureishi's comments that second-generation British-born Asians are able to blend the components of their hybrid existence: 'Far from being a conflict of cultures, our lives seemed to *synthesize disparate elements*: the pub, the mosque, two or three languages, rock 'n roll, Indian films. Our extended family and our British individuality *co-mingled*' (*MBL* 135; emphasis mine). It is significant that here Kureishi erases the conflict and unequal power relations inherent in the hybrid condition, when, as we have seen by his own admission, this harmonious synthesis does not reflect his personal, cultural background and nor is it the experience of many of his characters.

15. Bhabha's theories on hybridity cannot be summarized here. What is relevant is his idea of a hybrid 'Third Space' as an arena for cultural intervention and a way of conceptualizing cultural difference between the Third World (formerly colonized or migrant) cultures and First World cultures, sharing the same (metropolitan) space in the contemporary neo-colonial era. Bhabha suggests that the particular processes of cultural hybridity in the 'Third Space' can give rise to a new area of negotiation of meaning and representation: 'This third space displaces the histories that constitute it, and sets up new structures of authority, new political initiatives' see Homi Bhabha, 'The Third Space', in Jonathan Rutherford (ed.), *Identity, Community, Culture, Difference* (London: Law-rence and Wishart, 1990), 211.

16. Kureishi's delineations of the individual predicaments of Chad and Karim among others exemplify the pitfalls of cultural hybridity.

17. Nick Curtis, 'Radical Islam meets Ecstasy', *Financial Times*, 11 March 1995, XII.

18. Maya Jaggi, 'A Buddy from Suburbia', *Guardian*, 1 March 1995, 6–7.

19. Maya Jaggi makes this point in her review. Although she suggests that Kureishi's text 'treads carefully', she concludes that 'sadly that representation is hardly challenged in the novel'. Jaggi is one of the few voices of critique of this aspect of Kureishi's book. See Maya

Jaggi, 'A Buddy from Suburbia', *Guardian*, 1 March 1995, 6–7.

20. Tariq Modood, *Not Easy Being British: Colour, Culture and Citizenship* (London: Trentham Books Ltd.,1992), 87.

21. See Nikos Papastergiadis, 'Ashis Nandy: Dialogue and Diaspora', *Third Text*, 11 (1990), 100. See also Homi Bhabha, who argues that 'within the Shi'ite sect (which is too easily and too often read as "fundamentalist") there are a number of other positions' on the Rushdie Affair. These make a 'claim for a kind of hybridisation which exists no matter whether you keep asserting the purity of your origins'. See Homi Bhabha, 'The Third Space', in Rutherford (ed.), *Identity*, 214.

22. Akeel Bilgrami, 'What is a Muslim? Fundamental Commitment and Cultural Identity', *Critical Inquiry*, 18 (1992), 823. Tahira is the sole exception to this monolithic portrait: she points out the double standards of the brothers 'who urge [the women] to cover [themselves] but become strangely evasive when it comes to [their] own clothes' (*BA* 105).

23. Maya Jaggi, 'A Buddy from Suburbia', *Guardian*, 1 March 1995, 6–7.

24. Modood, *Not Easy Being British*, 29, 81.

25. Maya Jaggi, 'A Buddy from Suburbia' *Guardian*, 1 March 1995, 6–7.

26. Robert Stam and Ella Shohat, *Unthinking Eurocentrism* (London: Routledge, 1994), 215.

27. Cited in Harvey Porlock, 'Critical List', *Sunday Times*, 19 March 1995, Books section, 7.

28. Karen Robinson, 'Talking Books', *Sunday Times*, 4 August 1996, Books section, 10.

29. Donald Weber, '"No Secrets Were Safe from Me": Situating Hanif Kureishi', *The Massachusetts Review*, 38/1 (1997), 119, 129, 125, 127, 125.

30. Bobby Sayyid, *A Fundamental Fear: Eurocentrism and the Emergence of Islamism* (London: Zed Books, 1997), 17.

31. Kureishi says he was sure the scene of marital rape would be censored, but he wanted it included in the published version of the film. See Kenneth C. Kaleta, *Hanif Kureishi* (Austin, TX: University of Texas Press, 1998), 162.

32. Nigel Andrews, 'Cinema's Cinderella No More', *Financial Times*, 12 May 1997, 15.

33. Homi Bhabha, 'Unpacking my library…again', in Iain Chambers and Lidia Curti (eds.), *The Post-Colonial Question: Common Skies, Divided Horizons* (London: Routledge, 1996), 210.

34. Ibid., 208.

35. Ibid., 209–10.

36. Although, as Inderpal Grewal points out, 'unfortunately [Kureishi] does not ask the Pakistani women of Bradford what they want', as

she suggests, Kureishi's critique is important since such schools can 'concretize a reified "tradition" of the subordination of women', especially in the light of racism in Britain. For, as Black British feminists argue, this domination is sanctioned in terms of respecting Other cultures, which is another problem of liberalism. Inderpal Grewal, 'Salman Rushdie: Marginality, Women and Shame', in M. D. Fletcher (ed.), *Reading Rushdie: Perspectives on the Fiction of Salman Rushdie* (Amsterdam: Rodopi), 1994, 133. See Saeeda Khanum for an insightful account of some Muslim female pupils' views and of the way such schools are used to produce dutiful wives, in 'Education and the Muslim Girl', in Gita Sahgal and Nira Yuval-Davies, *Refusing Holy Orders: Women and Fundamentalism in Britain* (London: Virago, 1992), 124–40.

37. Homi Bhabha, 'Unpacking my library...again', in Chambers and Curti (eds.), *The Post-Colonial Question*, 209.
38. Modood, *Not Easy Being British*, 87.
39. Homi Bhabha, 'Unpacking my library...again', in Chambers and Curti (eds.), *The Post-Colonial Question*, 211.
40. Ibid., 211.
41. K. Anthony Appiah, 'Identity Crisis', *New York Times*, 17 September 1995, 42 (emphasis mine). To date Professor Akbar Ahmed is alone in his comments on the 'tired stereotypes' of the Muslim community in *My Son the Fanatic*, in 'Public purse funds distorted drama about Muslim condition', http//www.q-news.

CHAPTER 5. MID-LIFE CRISIS – VARIATIONS ON A THEME

1. Marlaine Glicksman, 'Interview' *Rolling Stone*, 19 November 1987, 33–4.
2. Kureishi, Cheltenham Literary Festival, 17 October 1997.
3. Colin MacCabe, 'Interview: Hanif Kureishi on London', *Critical Quarterly*, 41/3 (1999), 52 , 49, 52.
4. Sean O'Brien, 'Love in a Blue Time', *Times Literary Supplement*, 28 March 1997, 20.
5. Neil Berry, 'Conquerors of the Capital', *Times Literary Supplement*, 30 March 1990, 339.
6. Kureishi, Cheltenham Literary Festival, 17 October, 1997.
7. Ibid.
8. Lottie Moggach, 'How I Write', *The Times*, 16 January 1999, Metro section, 23.
9. Bruce Dessau, 'The Buddha of Bromley', in *Time Out*, Guide to The Word, 19 April 1999, 11.
10. Peter Kobel, 'Tilling the Fields of Conflicts Into Middle Ages', *New*

York Times, 20 June 1999, 11.

11. Lucy Johnston, 'Hanif and the Spurned Woman', *Observer*, 10 May 1998, 8.

12. Kureishi's mother and sister describe his claim to a working-class background in an interview as a distortion in an attempt to make his past more fashionable. See David Lister, 'Family at War', *Independent*, 8 May 1998, 17.

13. Farrah Anwar, 'Is There a Sodomite in the House?', *Guardian*, 7 August 1992, 29.

14. Paul Taylor, 'Sleep With Me', *Independent*, 1 May 1999, 39. Sarah Hemming, 'Kureishi's Whinge Too Far', *Financial Times*, 26 April 1999, 18.

15. Hanif Kureishi, 'Goodbye, Mother', *Granta*, 69 (Spring 2000), 99–141.

AFTERWORD

1. Heidi Safia Mirza (ed.), *Black British Feminism: A Reader* (London: Routledge, 1997), 9.

2. Meera Syal, personal communication, 12 February 2000.

3. Sukhdev Sandhu, 'Paradise Syndrome', *London Review of Books*, 18 May 2000, 34.

Select Bibliography

WORKS BY HANIF KUREISHI

Plays

Adaptation of Bertolt Brecht's *Mother Courage and her Children* (unpublished ms. first staged at the Barbican, 1984).
Outskirts and Other Plays, including *The King and Me, Outskirts, Borderline, Birds of Passage* (London: Faber and Faber, 1992).
Sleep With Me (London: Faber and Faber, 1999).

Screenplays

My Beautiful Laundrette (London: Faber and Faber, 1986).
Sammy and Rosie Get Laid (London: Faber and Faber, 1988).
London Kills Me (London: Faber and Faber, 1991).
My Son the Fanatic (London: Faber and Faber, 1997).

Novels

The Buddha of Suburbia (London: Faber and Faber, 1990).
The Black Album (London: Faber and Faber, 1995).
Intimacy (London: Faber and Faber, 1998).
Gabriel's Gift (London: Faber and Faber, 2001).

Short Stories

Most of his short stories were first published in *Granta*, the *New Yorker*, *London Review of Books, Harper's, Atlantic Monthly.*

'Esther', *Atlantic Monthly,* 263/5 (May 1989), 56–62.
Love in a Blue Time (London: Faber and Faber, 1997).
Midnight All Day (London: Faber and Faber, 1999).
'Goodbye, Mother', *Granta,* 69 (Spring 2000), 99–141.

Non-fiction

Kureishi writes for the *New Statesman and Society.*

'Dirty Washing', *Time Out*, 795 (14–20 November 1985), 25–6.
'Disposing of the Raj,' *Marxism Today* (January 1987), 43
'England Bloody England', *Guardian* (22 January, 1988) repr. in Kobena
   Mercer (ed.), *Black Film, British Cinema* (London: Institute of
   Contemporary Arts, 1988), 24–5.
'Some time With Stephen: 'A Diary' in *Sammy and Rosie Get Laid*
   (London: Faber and Faber, 1988.)
The Faber Book of Pop, ed. with Jon Savage (London: Faber and Faber,
   1995).
'The Rainbow Sign' (1986), 'Bradford' (1986), 'Finishing the Job' (1988),
   'Eight Arms to Hold You' (1991), 'Wild Women, Wild Men' (1992), in
   My Beautiful Laundrette and Other Writings (London: Faber and Faber,
   1996).
'The Boy in the Bedroom', see website www.HanifKureishi.com
Preface to the screenplay of *Intimacy*, forthcoming.

SELECTED INTERVIEWS

Collins, Glen, 'Screen Writer Turns to the Novel to Tell of Race and Class
   in London', *New York Times*, 24 May 1990, 17.
Dodd, Philip, 'Requiem for a Rave', *Sight and Sound*, 5/1 (1991), 9–11.
Douglas, Ginny, 'Sex and Spying in Suburbia', *Observer*, 1 April 1990, 65.
Glicksman, Marlaine, 'Interview' *Rolling Stone*, 19 November 1987, 33–4.
MacCabe, Colin, 'Interview: Hanif Kureishi on London', *Critical
   Quarterly*, 41/3 (1999), 37–56.
Pally, Maria, 'Kureishi Like a Fox', *Film Comment*, 22/5 (September–
   October, 1986, 50–55).
Root, Jane, 'Scenes from a Marriage', *Monthly Film Bulletin*, 52/622 (1985),
   333.
Singer, Elyse, 'Hanif Kureishi: A Londoner, But Not a Brit', in Melissa
   Biggs (ed.), *In the Vernacular: Interviews at Yale with the Sculptors of
   Culture* (Jefferson, NC: McFarland and Co., 1991), 103–9.
Treneman, Ann, 'Revelations: I Thought, I'll be a Writer', *Independent*, 15
   April 1997, 10.

CRITICAL STUDIES

Books on Kureishi

Kaleta, Kenneth C., *Hanif Kureishi: Postcolonial Storyteller* (Austin, TX: University of Texas Press, 1998). A comprehensive critical biography of Kureishi, examining his early plays up to *My Son the Fanatic*. It offers an insight into Kureishi's creative process and includes several personal interviews with Kureishi, as well as actors and producers who worked with him, and a useful bibliography.

Moore-Gilbert, Bart, *Hanif Kureishi* (Manchester: Manchester University Press forthcoming).

Books with Chapters, Sections or Essays on Kureishi

Gikandi, Simon, *Maps of Englishness* (New York: Columbia University Press, 1996).

hooks, bell, *Yearning: Race, Gender and Class Politics* (Boston: South End Press, 1991).

McLeod, John, *Beginning Postcolonialism* (Manchester: Manchester University Press, 2000).

Needham, Anuradha Dingwaney, *Using the Master's Tools: Resistance and the Literature of the African and South Asian Diasporas* (Houndmills: Macmillan, 2000).

Punter, David, *Postcolonial Imaginings*: *Fictions of a New World Order* (Edinburgh: Edinburgh University Press, 2000).

Spivak, Gayatri Chakravorty, *Outside in the Teaching Machine* (London: Routledge, 1993).

Articles

Alliot, Benedict, 'Misplacement in Hanif Kureishi's *The Buddha of Suburbia*', *Commonwealth Essays and Studies*, SP: 4 (1997), 95–100.

Ball, John, 'The Semi-Detached Metropolis: Hanif Kureishi's London', *Ariel*, 27/4, (1996), 7–27.

Carey, Cynthia, 'Hanif Kureishi's *The Buddha of Suburbia* as a Post-Colonial Novel', *Commonwealth Essays and Studies*, SP: 4 (1997), 119–25.

Chaudhuri, Una, 'The Poetics of Exile and the Politics of Home', in Patrick Hogan and Lalita Pandit (eds.), *Literary India*: *Comparative Studies in Aesthetics, Colonialism and Culture* (New York: State University of New York Press, 1995), 141–8.

de Cacqueray, Elisabeth, 'Constructions of Women in British Cinema: From Losey/Pinter's Modernism to the Postmodernism of Frears/

Kureishi', in *Caliban*, 32 (1995), 109–20.

Doyle, Waddick, 'The Space Between Identity and Otherness in Hanif Kureishi's *The Buddha of Suburbia*', *Commonwealth Essays and Studies*, SP: 4 (1997), 110–18.

Hall, Stuart, 'New Ethnicities', in Kobena Mercer (ed.), *Black Film, British Cinema* (London: Institute of Contemporary Arts, 1988), 27–30.

Hashmir, Alamgir, 'Hanif Kureishi and the Tradition of the Novel', *The International Fiction Review*, 19/2 (1993), 88–95.

Jena, Seema, 'From Victims to Survivors: The Anti-Hero and Narrative Strategy in Asian Immigrant Writing', *Wasafari*, 17 (Spring 1993), 3–6.

Lee, A. Robert, 'Changing The Script: Sex, Lies and Videotapes in Hanif Kureishi, David Dabydeen and Mike Philips', in A. Robert Lee (ed.), *Other Britain, Other British: Contemporary Multicultural Fiction* (London: Pluto Press, 1995), 69–89.

Misrahi-Barak, Judith, 'Yoga and the *Bildungsroman* in Hanif Kureishi's *The Buddha of Suburbia*', *Commonwealth Essays and Studies*, SP: 4 (1997), 88–94.

Mohanram, Radhika, 'Postcolonial Spaces and Deterritorialised (Homo)Sexuality: The Films of Hanif Kureishi', in Gita Rajan and Radhika Mohanram (eds.), *Postcolonial Discourse and Changing Cultural Contexts: Theory and Criticism* (Westport, CT: Greenwood Press, 1995), 117–34.

Moore-Gilbert, Bart, 'Hanif Kureishi and the Politics of Cultural Hybridity', in Jane Stokes and Anna Reading (eds.), *The Media in Britain: Current Debates and Developments* (Houndmills, Macmillan, 1999), 273–81.

Oubechou, Jamal, 'The Barbarians and Philistines in *The Buddha of Suburbia*', *Commonwealth Essays and Studies*, SP: 4 (1997), 101–9.

Rahman, Tariq, 'An Unresolved Confusion', *Dawn* (Lahore), 28 September 1990, pp. III–IV.

Ray, Sangeeta, 'The Nation in Performance: Bhabha, Mukherjee and Kureishi', in Monika Fludernik (ed.), *Hybridity and Postcolonialism* (Tübingen: Stauffenburg Verlag, 1998), 219–38.

Sandhu, Sukhdev, 'Pop Goes the Centre: Hanif Kureishi's London', in Laura Chrisman and Benita Parry (eds.), *Postcolonial Theory and Criticism* (Cambridge: D. S. Brewer, 2000), 133–54.

Schoene, Berthold, 'Herald of Hybridity: The Emancipation of Difference in Hanif Kureishi's *The Buddha of Suburbia*', *International Journal of Cultural Studies*, 1/1 (April 1998), 109–28.

Weber, Donald, '"No Secrets Were Safe from Me": Situating Hanif Kureishi', *Massachusetts Review*, 38/1 (1997), 119–35.

Yousaf, Nahem, 'Hanif Kureishi and "the Brown Man's Burden"', *Critical Survey*, 8/1 (1996), 14–25.

Index

Adebayo, Diran, 8
Ahmad, Rukhsana, 122
Amis, Martin, 112
Appiah, Kwame Anthony, 101

Baldwin, James, 3, 68
Barber, Frances, 52
Beatles, The, 63
Bellow, Saul, 11
Bhabha, Homi, 7, 87, 98–100,
    126 n. 33, 130 n. 30
Bhutto, Zulfikar Ali, 47
Black Panthers, 2
Bloom, Claire, 53
Brah, Avtar, 28
Braine, John, 10
Branche, Derek, 42
Brecht, Bertold, 60, 121
Butler, Judith, 69

Ceddo, 55
Chadha, Gurindher, 15, 114
Chadwick, Justin, 78
Chaudhuri, Nirad, 9, 13
Chekhov, Anton, 37
Chow, Rey, 126 n. 33
Collins, Merle, 8
Commission for Racial
    Equality, 82
Cornershop, 122

Davis, Angela, 66, 68
De Beauvoir, Simone, 68
Desai, Gopi, 93
Desani, G. V., 8
Devine, George, 23
Dhillon-Kashyap, Perminder,
    45, 48, 51
Dhondy, Farrukh, 34, 50
Din, Ayub Khan, 52, 122
Dodd, Philip, 79
Donnell, Alison, 16

Eliot, T. S., 58
Emin, Tracey, 120

Fanon, Frantz, 11
Fenton, James, 24, 34
Field, Shirley Anne, 42
Fielding, Henry, 8
Forster, E. M., 39
Frears, Stephen, 38, 40, 42, 50,
    52–4, 55, 58
Fusco, Coco, 14

Gazelle, Wendy, 52
Gift, Roland, 52
Gikandi, Simon, 4
Gilroy, Paul, 11, 68, 73–4
Gnew, Sneja, 50
Greer, Germaine, 68

145

Grewal, Inderpal, 48–9
Griffiths, Rachel, 93
Groce, Cherry, 52, 55

Hall, Stuart, 7, 16, 40–41, 51
Hardy, Thomas, 106
Hashmir, Alamgir, 10
Hebdige, Dick, 16, 28
Henriques, Julien, 42
Hirst, Damien, 120
hooks, bell, 55–6, 58–60
Hornby, Nick, 112

Jaggi, Maya, 88, 90
Jamal, Mahmood, 46, 49, 51
JanMohamed, Abdul, 13
Jaffrey, Saeed, 41
Jarrett, Cynthia, 52
Johnson, Linton Kwesi, 9
Julien, Isaac, 50

Kaleta, Kenneth, 10, 80
Kapoor, Shashi, 53
Kaye, M. M., 39
Kerouac, Jack, 11
Khomeini, Ayatollah, 83, 89
Kipling, Rudyard, 70, 72
Kureishi, Hanif
    Birds of Passage, 35–7
    Borderline, 18, 22, 25–35, 36–
        7, 56, 92, 105
    'Bradford', 83, 89
    Gabriel's Gift, 117–20
    Intimacy, 19–20, 77, 86, 102–
        3, 105, 109–14, 115–7
    London Kills Me, 17, 77–80,
        102, 118
    Love in a Blue Time, 17, 19,
        102–3, 105, 107–9, 116
    Midnight All Day, 19, 102,
        105, 114, 115–16
    My Beautiful Laundrette, 19,
        25, 33–4, 36–7, 38–52, 54,
        57–9, 77–8, 82, 89, 114–15,
        122
    My Son the Fanatic (film),
        81–3, 87, 93–8, 104, 121
    'My Son the Fanatic' (short
        story), 92–3, 102
    Outskirts, 22, 23–5
    Sammy and Rose Get Laid, 18,
        32, 34, 36, 38–41, 51–60,
        77–8, 85, 122
    Sleep With Me, 19, 102, 114–
        15
    The Black Album, 16–18, 29,
        32, 81–95, 98, 106, 119–20
    The Buddha of Suburbia
        (novel), 6–10, 16, 18, 27,
        29, 32–6, 61–77, 79, 84–5,
        103–4, 106, 114, 119–20,
        122
    The Buddha of Suburbia
        (film), 132 n. 3, n. 4, n. 6
    'The Rainbow Sign', 1–5,
        45, 56, 83, 103
    'Wild Women, Wild Men',
        98
Kurtha, Akbar, 93
Kymlicha, Will, 136 n. 11

Lawrence, D. H., 106
Lawrence, Stephen, 43
Lee, Spike, 67
Lewis, Daniel Day, 41

MacCabe, Colin, 53
Mackintosh, Steven, 78
Mailer, Norman, 11
McCourt, Emer, 78

Mehmood, Tariq, 50
Mercer, Kobena, 39, 50, 129 n. 20
Millet, Kate, 68
Mo, Timothy, 8
Modood, Tariq, 81–2, 89–90, 100
Muhammed, Elijah, 3

Naipaul, V. S., 8, 9, 12
Narayan, Uma, 51
National Front, 74
Needham, Anuradha Dingawaney, 4

Orton, Joe, 10, 76
Osborne, John, 10

Parma, Pratibha, 40
Phillips, Caryl, 8
Powell, Enoch, 2, 4, 22
Prasad, Udayan, 93
Presley, Elvis, 22
Puri, Om, 93

Quart, Leonard, 58

Riley, Joan, 8
Robbins, Harold, 76
Roth, Philip, 11
Royal Court Theatre, 10, 25
Rushdie, Salman, 3, 7, 8, 10, 12, 14–15, 39, 51, 81, 82–4, 87, 89, 98

Sahgal, Gita, 100
Said, Edward, 7
Salinger, J. D., 11
Sandhu, Sukhdev, 9, 78, 122

Savage, Jon, 15–16, 79
Scarman, Lord, 38
Scoffield, Tracey, 113
Scott, Paul, 39
Sellers, Peter, 65
Selvon, Sam, 8
Seth, Roshan, 43
Sex Pistols, The, 63
Sheridan, Richard, 10
Shohat, Ella, 45–7, 90
Singh, Talvin, 122
Sivandanan, Ambalavaner, 34
Smith, Zadie, 8
Spivak, Gayatri, 36, 43, 55, 67, 72
Stafford-Clarke, Max, 25
Stam, Robert, 45–7, 90
Sterne, Laurence, 8
Syal, Meera, 8, 15, 122, 129 n. 23

Taylor, Charles, 136 n. 11
Thatcher, Margaret, 21, 38–9, 52, 54–5, 57–8, 63
Theo-Goldberg, David, 31

Updike, John, 11

Warnecke, Gordon, 41, 122
Weber, Donald, 91
Wells, H. G., 19
Williamson, Judith, 50
Wilson, Angus, 11
Wolf, Rita, 42, 49, 122
Wright, Richard, 3

X, Malcolm, 3, 68

Yousaf, Nahem, 66